CONTENTS

EDINBURGH

WILLIAM RAE

CITY OF EDINBURGH DISTRICT COUNCIL

MAINSTREAM PUBLISHING

EDINBURGH AND LONDON

THE NEW
OFFICIAL GUIDE

The author and publishers would like to thank the following for
their help in the preparation of this book: National Galleries of
Scotland; the Royal Museum of Scotland; the National Portrait
Gallery (London); Historic Scotland; the Royal Highland and
Agricultural Society of Scotland; the Royal Botanic Garden; the
Edinburgh Military Tattoo; Edinburgh Zoo; Heriot-Watt
University; Edinburgh University; the Festival Fringe Office;
Murrayfield Racers; the Scottish Rugby Union; the Bridge Inn,
Ratho; the Traverse Theatre; the Edinburgh Room, Central
Library; and the Royal Observatory

Photographs by CEDC PR Division with contributions by
Graham Clark, David Morrison, Marius Alexander, Malcolm
Fife, Douglas Corrance and Fritz von der Schulenburg

This edition published by
CITY OF EDINBURGH DISTRICT COUNCIL
in conjunction with
MAINSTREAM PUBLISHING COMPANY
(EDINBURGH) LTD
7 Albany Street
Edinburgh EH1 3UG

ISBN 1 85158 605 9

A catalogue record for this book is available from the British
Library

Typeset in Plantin by Litho Link Ltd,
Welshpool, Powys, Wales
Printed in the EEC by Stiges

FOREWORD

*O*N behalf of all the citizens of Edinburgh may I welcome you to the ancient and historic capital of Scotland. Whether your visit is for business or pleasure I am sure you will enjoy your stay in Edinburgh and I trust this official guide will be an enjoyable souvenir of your time with us.

Throughout these pages you will see that the architecture of many ages is represented in the city, and I like to think that our history is written in the stones of our buildings as well as the achievements of our citizens, some of whom are featured throughout the guide.

Over many centuries Edinburgh has been one of the major cities of Europe, a status confirmed by our hosting of the European Council of Ministers meeting – the Euro Summit – in 1992.

Edinburgh is not just about history, however, important though that history is. The city has been and will continue to be a world leader in the sciences and particularly medicine, and we have a vibrant present and an exciting future as an international centre for the financial industry and for the arts.

Please enjoy your stay in Edinburgh and do tell all your family and friends about our beautiful city and the warm welcome that awaits them.

THE LORD PROVOST OF EDINBURGH,
THE RIGHT HONOURABLE NORMAN IRONS

Opposite: The Ross Fountain, West Princes Street Gardens

INTRODUCTION

EDINBURGH is the jewel in Scotland's crown. The jewel has many facets: classical architecture piled on hills, tree-filled valleys, sweeping Georgian crescents, medieval closes, graceful bridges soaring across chasms, green parks, sudden views of the sea from street corners. And the castle. That supreme castle, which looks so right that it might have grown out of the rock by some natural process.

The castle, older than Edinburgh itself, occupies a special corner of the Scottish folk memory. The fortress on the rock, the palladium of the city, remains a compelling symbol. It is a perpetual, very public reminder to Scots of their roots.

It has been said that Edinburgh often looks less like a modern city than a theatrical backdrop. This is true. On the visual level, Edinburgh is pure theatre. The basic reason, of course, is that Scotland's capital has the good fortune to be built upon hills.

The local topography is the result of the fact that Arthur's Seat was the principal volcano in this region millions of years ago. Much later, glacial action gouged a number of dramatic valleys in the landscape and shaped the high ridge on which the Old Town stands today.

The pedestrian in Edinburgh seldom walks on level ground: his day, like life itself, is a series of ups and downs. The gradients, however, are seldom steep, and the ideal way to see Edinburgh is on foot.

What is this life if, full of care,
We have no time to stand and stare?

Few cities offer more to those with a discerning eye. (For photographers it is a paradise.) Edinburgh's other great blessing is its architecture, whether Georgian, Victorian, Scots Baronial, medieval or whatever. Edinburgh has several thousand buildings that are officially protected because of their architectural or historic importance – more than any other city outwith London. A quarter of Scotland's A-listed buildings are in Edinburgh.

The eighteenth-century New Town is the largest area of Georgian architecture in Europe, and probably in the world: it has been officially recognised by the European Community as a valuable part of the European heritage. Edinburgh's blessing, then, has been the manner in which distinguished architects, particularly in the eighteenth and nineteenth centuries, endowed Edinburgh with a wealth of meritorious buildings – both public and private – and skilfully used Edinburgh's hills and valleys as a dramatic setting. Sir Walter Scott caught Edinburgh's magic on paper when he wrote:

Where the huge Castle holds its state,
And all the steep slope down,
Whose ridgy back heaves to the sky,
Piled deep and massy, close and high,
Mine own romantic town!

Previous page: The centre of Edinburgh

John Knox's House, High Street

Edinburgh people are very proud of their city and take the closest interest in their local environment. That is why so much that is worth while has survived, while other cities have bulldozed much of their heritage in pursuit of elusive improvement.

The intention behind this book is to introduce the visitor to the many attractions which Edinburgh people know and appreciate. Edinburgh people enjoy helping the stranger in their midst. Just ask.

Princes Street

National Gallery of Scotland, the Mound

Ramsay Garden, Castlehill

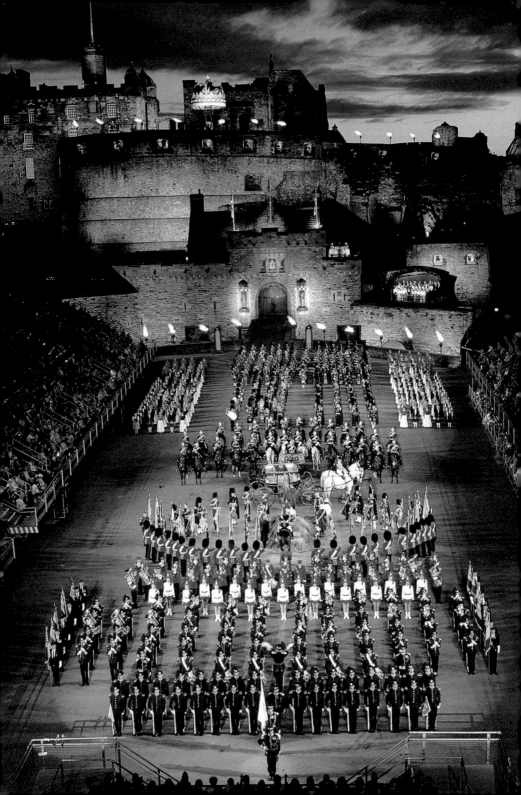

EDINBURGH CASTLE

THE CRAG WHERE EDINBURGH BEGAN

*T*HE castle is Edinburgh's best known and most popular visitor attraction. It is, therefore, a good idea (particularly if your stay in Edinburgh has to be brief) to visit the castle first.

For one thing, the magnificent panorama from the battlements will give you a splendid idea of the city and the surrounding terrain. It will be immediately apparent to history buffs, for example, why Edinburgh Castle was of strategic importance during Scotland's wars of independence.

Long before that, however, the precipitous rock, rising out of surrounding forest, is known to have been a tribal refuge and settlement. There is archaeological evidence of human habitation on the crag in the Bronze Age, about 1,000 BC. This evidence makes Edinburgh one of the longest continuously inhabited places in northern Europe.

Where did Edinburgh get its name? The answer is obscured by the mists of time.

The castle from the west

Opposite: Edinburgh Military Tattoo

The name could be a corruption of Edwin's Burgh, commemorating a ninth-century king of Northumbria, whose realm extended to the Firth of Forth. Other authorities, however, suggest that the original form of the city's name was 'din Eidyn' – this is Brythonic, a language akin to Welsh, spoken in the south-east of Scotland at the time.

Whatever doubts there may be about the name, the Castle Rock is undeniably where Edinburgh began. Early Edinburgh was a small settlement on the eastern side of the fortified rock, huddled close to the crag for protection. In the valley was a stretch of water, the Nor' Loch, which was developed in the fifteenth century as part of the town's defences. Three hundred years later, however, with the advent of more peaceful times, the loch was drained to make way for Princes Street Gardens.

Through the centuries, the castle was besieged many times, badly knocked about, held by the English as well as by the Scots, and well-nigh demolished more than once. But it always rose again. In that sense, the story of the castle is the story of Scotland.

Though the castle is a historic monument, it is also a working military establishment, being the headquarters of the Scottish Division: that is why there is a guard on the main gate.

One of the most evocative buildings within the castle is also the smallest and oldest – Saint Margaret's Chapel, built in the Norman fashion almost 1,000 years ago in honour of the saintly wife of King Malcolm III. Because of its religious significance, the tiny chapel survived every military demolition. After 900 years it is still in use, and members of the castle garrison may exercise their right to be married within it.

The castle was the seat of Scottish kings, and the royal apartments on view to the public include a tiny room in which Mary, Queen of Scots gave birth to the boy who became King James VI of Scotland and

James I of England upon the death of Queen Elizabeth I of England in 1603. Within the royal apartments a permanent exhibition, in the form of a series of impressive tableaux, depicts some of the milestones in Scotland's story.

The ancient Honours of Scotland – the crown, sceptre and sword of state – are on view in the Crown Room. One of the most romantic of the stories attached to the ancient crown jewels of Scotland concerns the manner of their rediscovery in 1818. It was known that, at the Treaty of Union in 1707, when the old Scots Parliament was dissolved for ever ('the end of an auld sang'), the Scottish Regalia had been deposited

The One o'Clock Gun

within Edinburgh Castle. No more appropriate resting-place for these revered relics of Scotland's sovereignty could have been found. As the years passed, there were disturbing rumours that the ancient regalia had been quietly removed to London. Eventually, largely by the intercession of that super-patriot Sir Walter Scott, authority was obtained from the Prince Regent (later George IV) in 1818 to make a search of the castle. In an oak chest within what is now the Crown Room, with Scott among the spectators, there was found the precious regalia, including the crown that had been made in the time of the great Bruce. Scott's emotions have been recorded by the historian James Grant: 'The joy was therefore extreme when, the ponderous lid having been forced open . . . the regalia were discovered lying at the bottom covered with linen cloths, exactly as they had been left in 1707.'

Today the ancient symbols of sovereignty are on permanent display to the people in that same room, where they saw the light of day once more almost two centuries ago. As one gazes upon the gleaming crown, sceptre and sword of state, it is not difficult to conjure up the drama of some earlier chapters of that 'auld sang'.

Nearby, in the Great Hall, which has an ornate wooden ceiling, there is an interesting collection of weapons and armour.

Across the square is the Scottish National War Memorial, a building designed by Sir Robert Lorimer and built shortly after the First World War. Few who walk round its interior fail to be moved by the experience. The graphic decoration speaks eloquently of the awful price that has been paid for our liberty.

On the western side of the square is the Scottish United Services Museum, which has an additional gallery in Hospital Square.

Near the summit of the castle a small, well-tended plot below the ramparts has served for many years as a cemetery for the pets of members of the garrison.

The castle is also the home of the most famous cannon in Scotland: Mons Meg, a massive fifteenth-century bombard, which was reputed to be able to fire a large stone cannonball a distance of one-and-a-half miles. Its devastating effect earned Meg the alternative name, 'the Muckle Murderer'. Salutes from the castle these days are fired by more modern artillery, when for example Her Majesty the Queen celebrates her birthday or enters Edinburgh on an official visit. Speaking of artillery, a unique institution within the castle is the One o'Clock Gun, which is fired at that hour every day (except Sunday) to enable citizens and visitors to check their clocks and watches. The origin of

the tradition lies in the days when sailing ships in the Firth of Forth were able to check their chronometers by training a telescope on the castle. Simultaneously, a time ball drops at the Nelson Monument on Calton Hill.

For three weeks in August each year the Castle Esplanade is the venue of the world-famous Edinburgh Military Tattoo, when the Scottish regiments host a lively programme of military music, marching and historical re-enactments under floodlights before large and appreciative audiences from all over the world.

Before leaving the esplanade, look for an artistically decorated drinking-well in the wall at the north-east corner. It is a grim reminder of the days when, on this spot, women, usually elderly, were executed by burning after having been convicted of practising witchcraft.

There is a more cheerful relic at Cannonball House, a few yards away at the top of the Castle Wynd steps. The building takes its name from a cannonball, embedded in the wall about halfway up. There are two legends, one military and one civil. The first story, which gunners dismiss as impossible, is that the cannonball was fired from the castle in 1745 and that it was aimed at Holyrood Palace, where Bonnie Prince Charlie was in residence during his march south (Edinburgh's allegiances were divided on this attempt by the Stuarts to regain the British throne).

The second, more prosaic story is that the cannonball was carefully placed here by engineers to mark the precise height above sea-level of the fresh springs at Comiston, in the hills to the south, which provided Edinburgh with its first piped supply of fresh water, in about 1621. Certainly the low building on the north side of the street was until recently a large water tank, serving the Old Town. Now, however, there are plans to use the redundant building for a tourism-related project.

PRINCES STREET

THE WORLD'S MOST HANDSOME BOULEVARD

*P*RINCES STREET, Edinburgh's main thoroughfare, has been described as one of the most beautiful streets in the world. Its fame springs, of course, not primarily from its architecture but from the street's incomparable setting. It is as fine a boulevard as will be encountered anywhere. Many of Edinburgh's best known shops have a Princes Street address, and the hotels can offer a magnificent prospect across the green valley of Princes Street Gardens to the high ridge of the Old Town, crowned by the castle.

For pedestrians who wish to escape the bustling traffic of Princes Street, it is literally only a few steps to the tranquillity of Princes Street Gardens. The gardens are in two parts, separated by the roadway of the Mound and the classical architecture of the art galleries.

In West Princes Street Gardens, look out for Edinburgh's famous floral clock

Castle Street

Opposite: Princes Street at dusk

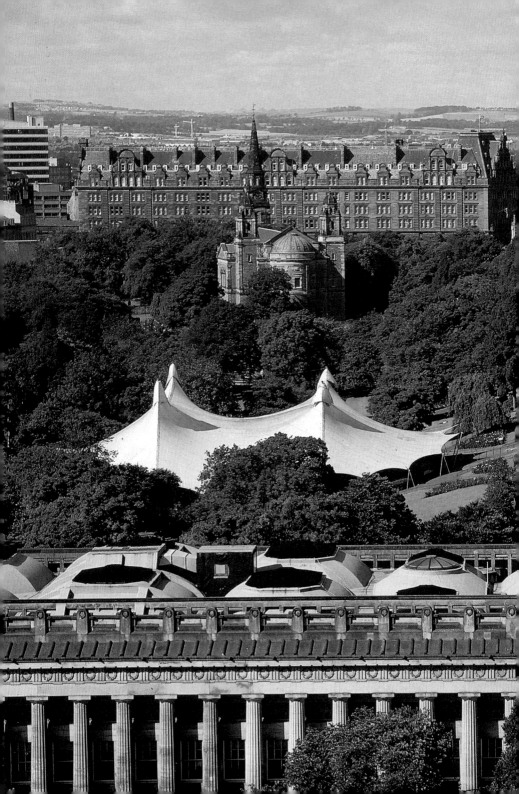

In the shadow of the Scott Monument

Scottish-American War Memorial: The Call

Previous page: Princes Street from the Scott Monument
Opposite: Piping a welcome on Princes Street

situated beside the flight of steps at the Mound entrance, below the statue of the poet Allan Ramsay. The oldest floral clock in the world, it is planted anew each spring with thousands of tiny plants. A mechanical cuckoo calls the hour.

On the upper promenade of West Princes Street Gardens is the Scottish–American War Memorial. Entitled 'The Call', the memorial's central feature is the seated figure of a young man in uniform, leaning forward, gazing intently towards the castle. The sculptor, the late R. Tait Mackenzie of Philadelphia, always maintained that he had modelled the evocative figure on a number of different sitters. Be that as it may, after the unveiling in 1927 many a grieving mother saw in the honest features the likeness of a son lost in the war.

Nearby is a heather garden, established following the Falklands conflict, and below in the valley is a peace garden, which includes a number of commemorative trees.

In the middle of West Princes Street Gardens stands the Ross Theatre, where a varied programme of entertainment is presented in the season, normally beneath the protection of a large canopy.

The massive boulder situated a short distance west of the Ross Theatre is a gift from the Norwegian people. It commemorates friendships forged during the Second World War, when large numbers of Norwegians, having been driven from their

EDINBURGHERS

Allan Ramsay the Younger

1713–84

PAINTER

•

The eldest son of the poet, Allan Ramsay excelled as a portrait painter, particularly of women.

After receiving training in Edinburgh and London, he went on to Italy and studied further there for some two years. He then made his name in London and was appointed portrait painter to George III, rather to the annoyance of the ambitious Sir Joshua Reynolds. Ramsay had charm, liked conversation, was popular in society and enjoyed travel, particularly in Italy.

His burial place is in Greyfriars Churchyard, Edinburgh. His work can be seen in the National Gallery at the Mound and in the Scottish National Portrait Gallery, Queen Street.

own land, found refuge, freedom and renewed hope in Scotland.

At the eastern end of the gardens stands the memorial of the oldest regiment in the British Army, the Royal Scots, inscribed with its long roll of campaign honours. The handsome equestrian statue, opposite Frederick Street, is the regimental memorial of the Royal Scots Greys.

The glorious prospect from Princes Street did not come about by chance: it was achieved by design, by public-spirited agitation and in the face of passionate debate about aesthetics and commercial prosperity. Eventually, in 1816, the authority of Parliament was obtained to safeguard for all time the radical concept of no building on the south side of Princes Street. It is because of this Parliamentary statute, in force now for nearly two centuries, that the art galleries at the foot of the Mound stand in splendid isolation. The same statute ensured that the prize-winning Waverley Market shopping centre (1985), at the east end of Princes Street, lies below pavement level.

The railway was introduced through Princes Street Gardens in 1846, but tunnelling and embankments, together with the well-wooded valley floor, have safeguarded the environment of the gardens. Railway passengers arriving from the west and north find themselves approaching Waverley Station through wooded parkland. Here is a further example of the way in which Edinburgh accepted the modern world, subdued a brash newcomer, and enlisted nature and time the healer to fit the railway into a unique urban environment.

In East Princes Street Gardens soars the 200-ft spire of the Scott Monument, Edinburgh's tribute to one of her illustrious native sons, the novelist and patriot Sir Walter Scott. The marble likeness of Scott at the base is by Sir John Steell; Scott's favourite dog, Maida, lies at his feet. Many characters from Scott's novels, as well as

The National Gallery

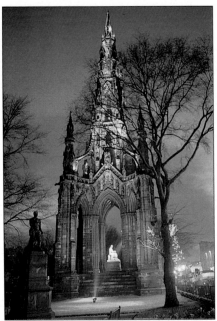

The Scott Monument

.The Ramsay Memorial on the Mound

Opposite: The city centre by night

figures from Scottish history, adorn the monument at various levels, and there is a small exhibition area halfway up. A circular stairway can be climbed to the top (287 steps in all) but those who lack the stamina can still enjoy a fine view by halting at intermediate stages.

The statue standing a few yards from the Scott Monument is that of David Livingstone, the Scots doctor/missionary/explorer who worked tirelessly in the African interior and who was located there by the intrepid H.M. Stanley in a famous encounter. Stanley, an American citizen, was made a freeman of Edinburgh on 11 June 1890.

The smallest memorial in East Princes Street Gardens, consisting of a bronze plaque embedded in stone near the northwest entrance, commemorates those volunteers who, as members of the International Brigades, fought on the Republican side during the bitter Spanish Civil War (1936–39).

The Waverley Market shopping centre, at the junction of Waverley Bridge with Princes Street, is admired for the interest of its interior design, which incorporates areas of water and much greenery.

On the roof of the shopping centre is the Edinburgh Information Centre – telephone no. (031) 557 1700. The centre provides information about Edinburgh exhibitions, special events, concerts and theatres, and sells tickets for some of the major entertainment venues, city bus tours, city walking tours, brewery tours, coach tours and Citylink bus travel. The centre has an accommodation booking service; a bureau de change is operated on the premises by the Clydesdale Bank; and a shop sells books and many other souvenirs. There is also an information desk at Edinburgh Airport for the assistance of visitors. There is a regular coach service between Edinburgh city centre (departing from Waverley Bridge) and the

Huge reductions on business flights from Edinburgh.

No longer do you have to go to the ends of the earth to travel the world. With regular, direct business flights from Edinburgh to Paris, Amsterdam, Brussels, as well as the London hubs, flying on to any number of worldwide destinations is easy. Just ask your travel agent about Edinburgh Airport and the incredible shrinking world.

B·A·A
Edinburgh Airport

East Princes Street Gardens

airport, journey time being approximately 25 minutes. Information about the timetable is available 24 hours a day by phoning (031) 220 4111. Adjacent to the Information Centre is Edinburgh's railway station, the Waverley, from which rail services are operated to all major centres throughout the United Kingdom.

Halfway along Princes Street is the Mound, an important road artery because it provides a convenient link between the New Town and the Old Town on the ridge. The Mound is man made, having been created in the eighteenth century with soil excavated during the building of the Georgian New Town. It is said that the Mound consists of two million cartloads of earth. At the time there was a big row about the dumping, and it certainly must have been an eyesore as it gradually blocked the valley, but landscaping and the passage of time have mellowed the argument.

At the foot of the Mound is the Royal Scottish Academy. Designed by William Henry Playfair (1789–1857), whose work adorns many parts of the city, the RSA is one of Edinburgh's artistic focal points. Behind the RSA is the National Gallery of Scotland, also by Playfair. The greater part of the permanent collection here consists of works by Continental and English masters.

A convenient flight of steps east of the National Gallery, leading from the pedestrian area up to Market Street, is named

Mound Precinct

after Playfair, whose classical designs were largely instrumental in Edinburgh being dubbed the 'Athens of the North'.

On the slope of the Mound is another Playfair creation, the Church of Scotland Assembly Hall, in which the General Assembly of the Kirk meets in May each year. In its courtyard is a powerful statue by John Hutchison of John Knox (1505–72), the thunderous father of the Reformation in Scotland. This whole area around the top of the Mound is typical of the Old Town, and its interesting lands and closes are worth exploring.

Also at the top of the Mound stand the offices of the Free Church of Scotland. Like the established Church of Scotland, the Free Church also meets in Edinburgh each May, its General Assembly being held in St Columba's on Johnston Terrace.

The handsome building on the slope above Market Street is the head office of the Bank of Scotland. As an institution, the bank began life (1695) elsewhere in the Old Town, moving to the present site in 1806. The present building (1870) by David Bryce is an enlarged and improved version of an earlier one by Robert Reid. A museum within the building contains an interesting selection of historic banknotes and coins, as well as a number of firearms which were in regular use at one time to protect the bank's valuable product as it travelled through the more lawless areas of Scotland.

At the summit of Market Street, the statue of a kilted soldier is the regimental memorial of the Black Watch. This was the regiment formed in the eighteenth century specifically to keep watch on the Highlands – their uniform was so dark as to appear almost black. The memorial was erected here following the South African War (1899–1902).

The Bank of Scotland Head Office

The Scott Monument

The Edinburgh Information Centre, Princes Street

CITY CENTRE MAP

1 Edinburgh Castle
2 Palace of Holyroodhouse
3 Scott Monument
4 High Kirk of St Giles
5 St Mary's Roman Catholic Cathedral
6 Tourist Information Centre
7 Waverley Rail Station
8 Bus Station
9 Tourist Buses
10 Greyfriars Bobby
11 Brass and Stone Rubbing Centre
12 Camera Obscura
13 John Knox's House
14 The Georgian House
15 Gladstone's Land
16 Royal Museum of Scotland, Chambers St
17 Royal Museum of Scotland, Queen St
18 The People's Story Museum
19 Huntly House Museum
20 Writers' Museum
21 Museum of Childhood
22 Royal Scottish Academy
23 National Gallery of Scotland
24 City Art Centre
25 Scottish National Portrait Gallery
26 King's Theatre
27 Royal Lyceum Theatre
28 Playhouse Theatre
29 Traverse Theatre
30 Netherbow Theatre
31 The Ross Open Air Theatre
32 MGM Film Centre
33 Odeon Film Centre
34 Cameo Cinema
35 Film House
36 Usher Hall
37 Queen's Hall
38 Assembly Rooms and Music Hall
39 St Cecilia's Hall
40 Ticket Centre
41 International Festival Office
42 Festival Fringe Office
43 Military Tattoo Office
44 Central Library
45 National Library of Scotland
46 Old College, University of Edinburgh
47 Royal Commonwealth Pool
48 Toilets
49 24 hour toilets
50 Toilets for disabled people
51 Carparks

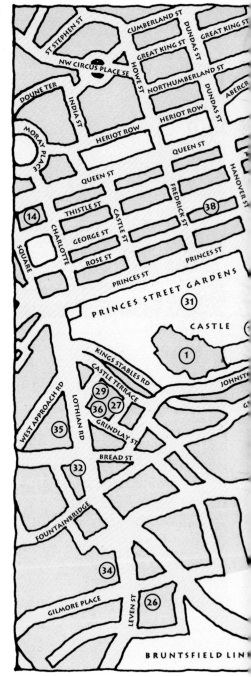

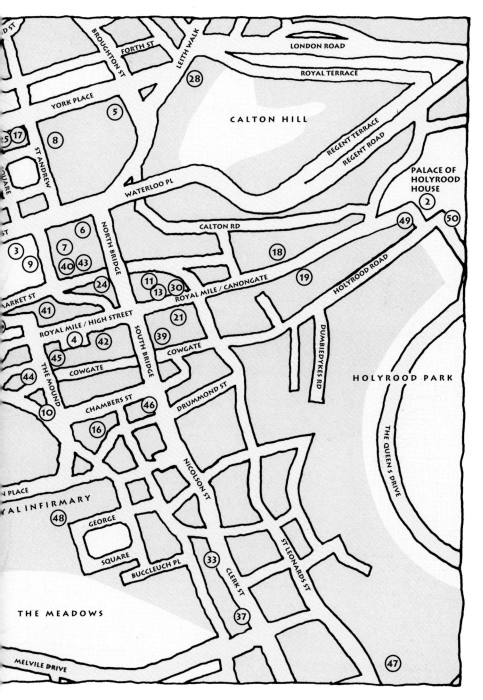

THE EAST END

A VIEW FROM THE BRIDGE

*W*HEN a city is built on hills, good bridges are crucial. Lord Provost George Drummond, the driving force behind Edinburgh's expansion in the eighteenth century, identified construction of a bridge across the valley to the north as a key element of the ambitious plan for a New Town.

The North Bridge that effortlessly leaps the valley today is not the original. The bridge is, however, a most impressive engineering feat, particularly when viewed from below. Those crossing the bridge on foot have a splendid vantage point from which to observe the castle, the Old Town front, Arthur's Seat, the Firth of Forth and the coast of East Lothian as far as Berwick Law.

The group of carved figures on the east parapet of the bridge is the regimental memorial of the King's Own Scottish Borderers, which commemorates those

The Old Town from Calton Hill

Opposite: Princes Street from the Scott Monument, looking east

EDINBURGHERS

David Octavius Hill

1802–70

PAINTER AND PHOTOGRAPHER

•

Landscape and portrait painter, D.O. Hill is nevertheless best known to history as a pioneer photographer. He was the first artist to apply the new invention of photography to portraiture, and many of the calotypes which he made of eminent figures are now a valued part of the national photographic archive. Hill had a studio on CALTON HILL, and was closely associated in his photographic work with Robert Adamson, of St Andrews.

In the FREE CHURCH ASSEMBLY HALL, Edinburgh, is a historic picture by Hill, containing no fewer than 500 portraits of all the leading lay and clerical members who demitted from the Church of Scotland at the Disruption in 1843. The picture shows the act of signing the deed of demission, and it took Hill more than 20 years to make all the portraits.

Hill is buried in the Dean Cemetery, Edinburgh, where there is a bronze bust of him by his widow.

members of the regiment who fell in a number of campaigns, culminating in the South African War.

At the north end of the bridge, the East End of Princes Street is one of the city's most important junctions. It is fitting, therefore, that it should be the site of Register House, one of the finest buildings of Robert Adam. It was begun in 1774 as the depository of Scotland's records, and though these voluminous records have of necessity now overflowed into a number of additional buildings, Register House remains the admired heart of the system. Exhibitions held regularly in Register House offer an opportunity to see the fine dome.

The impressive bronze equestrian statue immediately outside is of the Duke of Wellington, victor of the Battle of Waterloo and successful prime minister. The sculptor was Sir John Steell, so the new statue was soon dubbed 'the Iron Duke in bronze by Steell'. The Duke is pointing across the street to the General Post Office.

The British Philatelic Bureau, which was established by the Post Office in 1963, moved to Edinburgh three years later and is now at 20 Brandon Street, Canonmills. The bureau provides new British stamps and related items to more than a quarter of a million regular customers in over 130 countries.

At the top of Leith Street stands the St James Centre, a massive, modern shopping centre recently refurbished. Within the same complex is New St Andrew's House, which is a headquarters of the Scottish Office and the administrative heart of the central government's operations in Scotland.

Attractive architecture on a more human scale can be discovered in the neighbourhood. On the west side of Register House, for example, pedestrian walks and modest streets will lead one to such interesting public houses as the Guildford Arms

Doulton tiles in the Café Royal Bar

The Old Town from the north

Paolozzi sculpture, Picardy Place

and the Café Royal. In the latter, the visitor should note the series of remarkable Doulton tiles on the wall: they were made especially for the Edinburgh International Exhibition of 1886 and subsequently acquired by the Café Royal.

Near the junction of Picardy Place and York Place is St Mary's Roman Catholic Cathedral. A few yards from the cathedral are three major sculptures by Sir Eduardo Paolozzi, Her Majesty's Sculptor-in-Ordinary in Scotland, who was born and brought up in Leith. These bronze works, which include a giant-sized hand and foot, were installed here in 1991. Inscribed on the foot is a medieval Latin lyric, which was chosen by the sculptor to symbolise the ties between Italy and Scotland, represented by generations of Italian families who have made their home here.

On the north side of the Picardy Place roundabout stands a fine bronze statue of Sherlock Holmes, the legendary detective, complete wth cape, pipe and deerstalker. The statue, the only one of Holmes in Britain, is by Gerald Ogilvie Laing and was commissioned by local members of the Federation of Master Builders to mark their 50th anniversary and in tribute to Holmes' creator, Sir Arthur Conan Doyle, who was born at no. 11 Picardy Place. The statue was unveiled in June 1991.

Incidentally, Picardy Place derives its name from the fact that French Protestant refugees, silk weavers, settled in this neighbourhood of Edinburgh after fleeing from religious persecution in Picardy in 1685.

On the east side of the roundabout, the Playhouse Theatre is the venue for all kinds of entertainment, from pop concerts to opera, from films to ballet.

33

Register House at the east end of Princes Street

CASTLEHILL AND LAWNMARKET

THE WYNDS AND CLOSES OF THE OLD TOWN

*O*N leaving the Castle Esplanade we immediately enter the Royal Mile. This is the popular name given to the fascinating string of historic streets which, linking the two royal residences of castle and Holyrood Palace, was *the* thoroughfare of medieval Edinburgh. The Royal Mile was where the action was! Here you would find street stalls, taverns, royal processions, thieves, street entertainers, beggars, public hangings, riots, the unpopular Town Guard, soldiers from the castle, merchants, foreigners, fine town houses of the nobility, and the law courts.

Today the Royal Mile retains its distinctive character, thanks to a durable architectural profile and a policy of careful conservation. The rehabilitation of many of the area's historic buildings as residences during the past 60 years has provided a firm foundation for a thriving modern community.

A view from Salisbury Crags

Sir Patrick Geddes

1854–1932
PLANNER

•

A Scot who has been called the father of modern town planning, Geddes did much of his pioneering work in the Old Town of Edinburgh, having made his married home there in 1886. Geddes' name and spirit are imperishably associated with RAMSAY GARDEN and the OUTLOOK TOWER, both in Castlehill. He acquired the Outlook Tower in 1892, and it became the nerve centre from which his enlightened ideas on civics and country and town planning radiated.

In his Outlook Tower Geddes presented interpretations of city, region, continent and world: the message was that life had to be seen as a whole, with many sides in proper relation to each other. In planning, Geddes placed great emphasis on the importance of fostering neighbourhood and community.

In 1911 he created a milestone exhibition, Cities and Town Planning, which was studied appreciatively not only throughout Britain but also abroad. From 1920–23 he was Professor of Civics and Sociology at the University of Bombay, and in 1924 he settled at Montpellier, in France. He died there in 1932, having been knighted that year.

It is not difficult in the Old Town to sense an earlier age, particularly when wandering the many narrow closes and wynds that run at right angles from the Royal Mile. These closes, every one of which has a tale attached to it, usually open into courtyards, characteristic of a bygone lifestyle. Different social classes often were neighbours in these tenement buildings, which had a common entrance from the public street.

In the early years of the present century, a period when much of the Old Town had deteriorated to slum property, many a destitute family still sat by an ornate fireplace inscribed with the coat of arms of a half-forgotten noble family.

At the very top of the Royal Mile is Castlehill, a fairly short street in which one of the most interesting buildings is the Outlook Tower. It is one of a number in this immediate area associated with Sir Patrick Geddes (1854–1932), a Scot who has been called the father of modern town planning. Geddes' enlightened ideas and practical teaching, particularly about urban living, had great influence, not only in Scotland but far beyond these shores, including France, the Middle East and India.

At the top of the Outlook Tower is the famous Camera Obscura, installed in 1853. In a dark chamber, the camera's system of revolving lenses and mirrors projects a moving image of the surrounding city before the audience, while the operator tells the story of the city's historic past.

Opposite: Memorial to Field Marshal Earl Haig, Castle Esplanade

EDINBURGHERS

Sir Walter Scott

1771–1832
WRITER
•

Scott was born in Edinburgh and from an early age began to explore the country, listening avidly to Scottish songs and stories. Called to the bar at 21, he served on the bench as sheriff depute for a spell before being appointed a clerk of session in 1806. In the previous year he had published his long poem, 'Lay of the Last Minstrel'. The novel *Waverley* was published anonymously in 1814, and his prose output thereafter was prodigious – something like 23 books in 12 years. Scott's novels were immensely popular, not only in this country. He was deeply patriotic, and his writing is credited with having rekindled the embers of Scottish national sentiment. His Edinburgh home during this period was at no. 39 NORTH CASTLE STREET. In 1826 the business failure of Scott's publisher, John Ballantyne (with whom Scott was in partnership) precipitated the great crisis in the author's life. Characteristically he vowed to repay the creditors by means of his writing. Scott became a literary workaholic. In heroically tackling what seemed an impossible task, Scott undermined his health, and seven years later he died at his beloved Abbotsford, in the Borders. He did, however, achieve his honourable goal, for the last of his debts were cleared with sums realised on the security of copyright of his popular works.

Make a brief detour down Ramsay Lane to have a look at the charming exterior of Ramsay Garden, a property which Geddes developed carefully around an older core of buildings that includes the 'Goose-pie', the octagonal home of the poet Allan Ramsay (1686–1758). The commanding situation of Ramsay Garden, at the summit of Princes Street Gardens, gives these residential flats an incomparable view of Edinburgh.

The story of Scotch whisky is entertainingly explored at the Scotch Whisky Heritage Centre, at 354 Castlehill. During a visit lasting about one hour, the visitor steps back into history and sees the development of this famous beverage through the centuries. Travelling in an electric barrel car, the visitor makes a journey of discovery through the social and industrial history of whisky.

At the junction of Castlehill and Johnston Terrace soars Tolbooth St John's, a church designed by Augustus Pugin. Its tremendous yet graceful spire will be found in most of Edinburgh's famous skylines.

The Lawnmarket, whose name is thought to indicate the recognised centre in olden times for trading in linen, offers a good example of the system of closes, tenemented 'lands' and courtyards that characterise the Old Town.

The most notorious denizen of this neighbourhood was Major Thomas Weir, who in the seventeenth century lived in the West Bow with his sister, Grizel. Weir, though a grim-looking figure, was outwardly a pious man, and highly thought of for his devout prayers and powerful preaching. Wrapped in his long cloak, he would habitually lean on a staff while delivering his sermons. There was, therefore, stunned disbelief when he broke down and confessed to the most revolting crimes. Grizel confessed to practising witchcraft. People swore that the major's staff had a life of its own,

Mylne's Court, Lawnmarket

The Writers' Museum, Lawnmarket

carrying out his orders and proceeding down the Lawnmarket independently of its master. After his trial in 1670, during which the evidence was sensational, Major Weir was convicted of sorcery and sentenced to be strangled and burnt; Grizel was hanged in the Grassmarket. The wizard's staff was consigned to the flames with its master but, it is said, was consumed only with difficulty.

On the north side of the Lawnmarket is Mylne's Court. Named after its architect, master mason to Charles II, it is among the oldest surviving in Edinburgh and conveys the modest scale upon which life in the Old Town was lived. Today the interiors of these buildings have been modernised to provide residential flats for students of Edinburgh University.

More spacious is nearby James Court, which houses the Writers' Museum. This interesting house dates from 1622. In the eighteenth century it was the home of Lady Stair, the widow of the first Earl of Stair. Today it is the municipal museum principally known for its collection of artefacts associated with three Scottish men of letters – Sir Walter Scott, Robert Louis Stevenson (both natives of Edinburgh) and Scotland's national bard, Robert Burns. Burns lodged only a few yards away, in the Lawnmarket, during one of his successful visits to the Scottish capital – there is a commemorative plaque above street level.

Also on this side of the Lawnmarket is Gladstone's Land, owned by the National Trust for Scotland. Built by Thomas Gledstanes, it is well worth visiting as a skilfully restored example of a merchant's house of the seventeenth century. Interesting painted ceilings are one of its features.

On the other side of the street is Riddle's Court, which dates from the sixteenth century and is noted for the stair tower in its inner courtyard. A pend leads to Bailie McMorran's House (sixteenth century), the home of a leading citizen of the

The Scotch Whisky Heritage Centre

time. His name is best remembered today for the manner of his death: a magistrate, he proceeded to the Royal High School to quell a riot among the students in 1595 and was shot dead by one of the schoolboys. So much for the myth of superior classroom discipline in the old days.

Also on the south side of the Lawnmarket is Brodie's Close. It is named after a respectable craftsman, Francis Brodie, but it is his son, William, whose name and deeds everyone remembers. This is because William Brodie, ostensibly a respectable member of the Town Council, was discovered to be a professional burglar on a grand scale. Deacon Brodie was unmasked as the result of an unsuccessful armed raid on the Excise Office

at Chessel's Court, off the Canongate. Brodie managed to escape to Holland but was arrested there, brought back for trial, convicted and hanged in public in the High Street in 1788.

The final irony was that Brodie was executed with an improved version of the gallows which he invented. Deacon Brodie's nefarious career made a lasting impression, shown by the fact that the largest public house in the Lawnmarket is named after him. Robert Louis Stevenson, in writing *The Strange Case of Dr Jekyll and Mr Hyde*, was inspired either by Deacon Brodie's double life, or by the case of that even more sinister character, Major Weir.

GREYFRIARS

THE STORY OF GREYFRIARS BOBBY

*G*REYFRIARS KIRK, whose entrance gates stand near the south end of George IV Bridge, is one of Edinburgh's most historic churches. The churchyard, a pleasant green space, has an air of tranquillity that belies its location in the heart of the busy city. This is Edinburgh's oldest graveyard, and it has numerous associations with the history of the town and, indeed, of Scotland.

The original Greyfriars was a Franciscan friary, now long gone. The present church, belonging to the Church of Scotland, dates from 1620 and was the first new church to be erected in Edinburgh after the Reformation. The National Covenant, that militant expression of the Presbyterian faith, was signed in the church in 1638. There is another reminder of Scotland's troubled ecclesiastical history in the presence of a memorial to those Covenanters who were imprisoned here, under conditions of great hardship, for their religious beliefs.

Greyfriars Churchyard

Immediately outside the churchyard gates, at the crest of Candlemaker Row, stands the celebrated bronze likeness of Greyfriars Bobby. This is perhaps the most famous memorial to a dog to be found anywhere. For more than a century now, this true story has had an extraordinary hold on public sentiment; moreover, the story now seems to be as well known abroad as it is in this country, to judge by the numbers of knowledgeable visitors seen being photographed beside the monument.

In 1858 this faithful Skye terrier followed the remains of his master, John Gray, to Greyfriars churchyard. After the interment, the dog refused to leave the graveside.

For the next 14 years, until his own death, Bobby was never far from the churchyard. A shelter was constructed there for him, and he was given his food regularly in the kitchens of dining rooms nearby. When the question of his licence arose, the lord provost of the day paid it personally.

The touching story of the little dog's fidelity spread throughout the land. Travellers went to the churchyard especially to observe the famous Bobby. One of these, the philanthropist Baroness Burdett Coutts, was so impressed that she was instrumental in having the statue sculpted. The monument was unveiled in 1873, not long after Greyfriars Bobby died. He is now buried within the churchyard.

Sculpture, Greyfriars Churchyard

Opposite: The Grassmarket

George IV Bridge is one of those very well disguised Edinburgh bridges that pass themselves off as an ordinary street. The secret is revealed halfway along its length, when the stranger sees for the first time that he is actually on a high bridge, gazing down upon fast-moving traffic in the Cowgate far below. It is another of those little surprises that regularly confront and reward the stroller in Edinburgh.

George IV Bridge is also the address of two of the most important libraries in Edinburgh – two vast literary repositories directly facing each other. The Central Public Library, founded just over 100 years ago through the generosity of Dunfermline-born Andrew Carnegie, has extensive collections of books for borrowing and reference, including special collections on music and the fine arts. There is a Scottish department, and (a unique facility) the Edinburgh Room: its maps, prints, photographs, books, periodicals, newspapers and press cuttings trace the history of Edinburgh from the earliest times. Visitors may use the lending facilities by arrangement.

Directly across the street is the National Library of Scotland, which though in a modern building was founded in 1682 and is one of the UK's copyright deposit libraries. With some 4,500,000 books and an extensive collection of manuscripts, it is one of the largest libraries in Great Britain. Its map collection is among materials now available in a modern annexe at Causewayside.

Another important edifice in this area is the Royal Museum of Scotland in Chambers Street. The museum houses the national collections of decorative arts of the world, archaeology, ethnography, natural history, geology, technology and science. Its displays range from primitive art to space-age materials, and its working models in the Hall of Power are a source of perpetual fascination, particularly among the young. There are also regular programmes of temporary exhibitions, lectures, films and talks.

Greyfriars Bobby's memorial

The building, which was designed by Captain Francis Fowke of the Royal Engineers, has been described as one of the finest examples of Victorian architecture in Edinburgh. It was begun in 1861 and completed in 1888. The central hall is notable for the slender grace of its soaring cast-iron columns. An extension being built to the west is due to be completed in 1997.

On the other side of Chambers Street, the handsome nineteenth-century building (formerly the home of Heriot-Watt University) has been adapted to form part of a new Sheriff Court. New construction in the Cowgate at the rear provides accommodation for the Crown Office.

The statue in the middle of Chambers Street is of William Chambers, lord provost from 1865 to 1869, who led a campaign for improvement of public health in the Old Town.

Opposite: The Royal Museum of Scotland, Chambers Street

SOME PEOPLE COME INTO OUR BANK JUST TO LOOK AT THE CEILING.

Hardly surprising. Dundas House in the highly prestigious St Andrew Square, was built in 1772 when one Edinburgh chronicler noted that it was 'incomparably the handsomest house we ever saw'. The 1860 Banking Hall behind it is no less splendid.

Come along and see for yourself, we'i open to both customers and visitors durin banking hours.

The Royal Bank of Scotland

The Royal Bank of Scotland plc. Registered Office: 36 St Andrew Square, Edinburgh EH2 2YB. Registered in Scotland No 903

THE GRASSMARKET AND THE COWGATE

EDINBURGH'S MARKET PLACE

*F*OR at least 500 years the Grassmarket has been an important focal point of the Old Town.

It has been a trading place since the earliest times. The first written record of a market there is in 1477, and the tradition of this weekly event survived into the early years of the present century. By that time, a greatly expanded city and modern trading practices dictated the need for purpose-built markets outwith the confines of the city centre.

One of the most attractive things about the Grassmarket today is that it is immediately recognisable as a market-place. Buildings rise up on all four sides, enclosing a large open area overlooked by the towering castle. An examination of paintings of old Edinburgh shows that the historic Grassmarket has always been a favourite

St Patrick's Roman Catholic Church, Cowgate

The West Port

Solicitors' Buildings, Cowgate

spot for artists in search of the picturesque.

Historical associations abound. At the east end of the Grassmarket, near the foot of Victoria Street, a small garden, a plaque, and stone markers in the centre of the roadway commemorate the place of execution where many Covenanters were put to death because they would not renounce their Presbyterian faith.

Victoria Street is still known to local folk as the West Bow, which once was a steep, twisting street leading up to the top of the Royal Mile and Castlehill.

It was in the Grassmarket in 1736 that an Edinburgh mob lynched Captain Porteous, the commander of the Town Guard. Porteous had ordered the guard to fire upon a crowd with fatal results. He was put on trial and convicted of murder – but then he received a reprieve from London. Incensed, the mob dragged Porteous from the Old Tolbooth, which stood in the Royal Mile near St Giles', purchased a rope in the West Bow, and hanged him in the Grassmarket from a dyer's pole.

There are elements of mystery in the affair, in that it is said the abduction and hanging were carried out with orderliness and some evidence of organisation (a guinea was left on the shop counter to pay for the rope) and the crowd dispersed immediately after the fatal deed.

In London Queen Caroline, the wife of George II, was acting as Regent during the King's absence in Hanover. The news of Porteous's death infuriated the Queen, who made all sorts of dire threats, including abolition of the city charter. However, she was eventually persuaded to substitute a fine.

On the north side of the Grassmarket, one of the hostelries is the White Hart Inn, where Robert Burns found lodgings in 1791 during his final visit to Edinburgh. It was during this visit that his farewell to 'Clarinda' (Mrs Agnes MacLehose) inspired him to compose 'Ae Fond Kiss'. In 1803 another poet, William Wordsworth, and his sister Dorothy, stayed at the White Hart during the course of their travels in Scotland.

The Grassmarket was also the haunt of the infamous murderers Burke and Hare. During 1827 and 1828 they suffocated close on a score of men and women in their lodgings in Tanner's Close, in the nearby West Port, as a way of providing cadavers for the university's lecturing anatomists, who didn't ask too many questions. Burke was hanged at the Lawnmarket; Hare escaped the rope, having turned King's evidence after their arrest.

At the western end of the Grassmarket, the name of King's Stables Road recalls that this was the area in which the royal stables attached to the castle once stood. And in the Vennel, leading by a flight of steps to Lauriston, it is still possible to see a stretch of the Flodden Wall, hurriedly constructed by the town following the disaster on Flodden Field in 1513, when it seemed likely that the English would follow up their victory with the sacking of Edinburgh. At this point the wall forms the boundary of George Heriot's School, which was founded by Heriot (1563–1624), a jeweller who was also banker to King James VI and, as a result, known as Jinglin' Geordie.

On leaving the Grassmarket at its eastern end we enter the Cowgate. The line of this ancient thoroughfare, once a path along which cows were driven to pasture, follows the south flank of the Old Town ridge as far as St Mary's Street. Centuries ago the Cowgate was a fashionable quarter of the town, but by the early nineteenth century its status had deteriorated badly, and its profile subsequently was altered out of all recognition when encroached upon by new building.

Bannerman's in the Cowgate

EDINBURGHERS

James Boswell

1740–95
WRITER
•

Best remembered today as friend and biographer of Dr Samuel Johnson, Boswell was an extraordinary figure of eighteenth-century society. Vain yet good-natured, foolish yet charming, he was also conceited and a hypochondriac with a drinking problem. He forced himself upon eminent people, and bragged about the great men he knew. David Hume thought him a bit crazy. Yet for years Boswell moved in the same circles as Sheridan, Goldsmith, Rousseau, Voltaire and Walpole. And he was an inveterate notetaker.

Boswell, born in Edinburgh, was the son of Alexander Boswell, an advocate who some years later was elevated to the bench of the Court of Session and took the judicial title of Lord Auchinleck, after the family estate in Ayrshire. At the University young James studied law but his heart was never in it – to his father's irritation he preferred high life in London and travel in Europe.

In London, Boswell ('Bozzy' to all his friends) shamelessly badgered his contacts for an introduction to Dr Johnson. When they eventually met in 1763, the two men rapidly became friends. From the very first, the young Scot made notes of the great man's conversation, Johnson encouraging him to do so.

Boswell married in 1769. His wife was a sensible woman and extraordinarily patient with her gadabout husband. She did not share his enthusiasm for Johnson.

Boswell entertained Johnson in James Court, Lawnmarket, in 1773 when the great man arrived in Edinburgh to begin their famous journey to the Hebrides. Boswell's *Journal of a Tour to the Hebrides* was not published until 1786, a year after Johnson's death. His *Life of Samuel Johnson*, published in 1791, was an immediate success.

A perceptive observer blessed with a retentive memory, Boswell's narrative has dramatic power. These gifts and his industry have given us an incomparable picture of his times.

A few interesting fragments remain. Magdalen Chapel, for example, was completed in 1544, and at the Scottish Reformation the chapel was the meeting place of the first General Assembly of the Church of Scotland, held in 1560. It contains the only surviving examples of pre-Reformation stained glass in Scotland. The chapel has been undergoing careful restoration and is now the headquarters of the Scottish Reformation Society. It is open to the public from Monday to Friday, 9.30 am to 4.30 pm but can also be opened at other times by arrangement: phone the Rev. Sinclair Horne on (031) 220 1450.

St Cecilia's Hall (1763), which is owned by the Department of Music of Edinburgh University, is a charming concert hall in the Cowgate. It is in use regularly for a variety of concerts and other events, and it is also the home of the Russell Collection of Harpsichords and Clavichords. This is an assembly of more than 30 historical keyboard instruments, including also forte-pianos, spinets, virginals and chamber organs. It is also possible to visit the Edinburgh University Collection of Historical Musical Instruments at the Reid Concert Hall, Bristo Square: the display consists of 1,000 items, including stringed, woodwind, brass and percussion instruments, as well as some folk instruments.

THE UNIVERSITIES

EDINBURGH, HERIOT-WATT AND NAPIER

THERE are no fewer than three universities in Edinburgh – the University of Edinburgh (founded 1583), Heriot-Watt University (1966) and Napier University (1992).

The first of these, which was one of Scotland's medieval seats of learning, was founded by the Town Council of Edinburgh. Today it has more than 10,000 students and 1,500 staff. In the present century it has spread over a considerable geographical area, but it is fair to say that its heart remains the Old College, in South Bridge. It is not generally realised that students represent 25 per cent of the population of the Old Town.

The Old College, built in the classic style with a large quadrangle at its centre, was designed by Robert Adam and begun in 1789. Following Adam's death it was completed by William Henry Playfair. The large dome, one of the landmarks of the city

McEwan Hall, Bristo Square

·EDINBURGHERS

Robert Adam

1728–92

ARCHITECT

•

Robert Adam is renowned for his fine buildings, both public and private, in classical style throughout Britain. In Edinburgh his works include REGISTER HOUSE, the north side of CHARLOTTE SQUARE, and ·EDINBURGH UNIVERSITY OLD COLLEGE. The magnificent HOPETOUN HOUSE, at Queensferry, has been described as Scotland's greatest Adam mansion.

Adam, who was born in Kirkcaldy, regularly worked in conjunction with his architect brothers, John, James and William. They were responsible for much Georgian development in London, particularly town housing that took the form of elegant terraces.

Robert became architect to George III, and with James designed a number of important mansions in different parts of the country. Robert Adam is buried in Westminster Abbey.

centre, is by Sir Rowand Anderson and was added in 1883. The Old College building contains the Upper Library, generally regarded as one of the finest rooms in Edinburgh.

Also within the Old College is the Talbot Rice Art Centre, which houses the Torrie Collection, a permanent display of sixteenth- and seventeenth-century European painting and sculpture in Playfair's magnificent gallery. The Talbot Rice centre is also a venue for temporary exhibitions.

The university has faculties of arts, divinity, law, medicine, music and science. The medical school has a worldwide reputation. It was founded about 1690, but the present buildings in Teviot Place are nineteenth century, as are many of the other university buildings in the area. The McEwan Hall (1897), by Sir Rowand Anderson, is a fine example.

In the present century the university has also developed on two additional sites – at King's Buildings, West Mains, to which the faculty of science moved in 1928; and in George Square, after the Second World War, when the university erected a number of high-rise buildings that provoked heated argument at the time.

Heriot-Watt University, whose spacious, modern campus is at Riccarton, to the west of the city, was incorporated in 1966 but possesses a long technological pedigree. Founded in 1821 as a School of Arts and Mechanics Institute, it became in 1854 the Watt Institution and School of Arts, and from 1885 was the Heriot-Watt College until its elevation to university status in 1966.

Its Science Park has a close working relationship with commerce, having pioneered Britain's first research park for use by both industry and the university. Many of the Heriot-Watt students come from abroad (there is a strong connection with Norway, for example).

Napier University (1992) began life as

Opposite: Old College, South Bridge

Napier College of Science and Technology in 1964. Located in a number of buildings in the south and west of the city – Merchiston, Craiglockhart, Marchmont, Morningside and Sighthill – Napier is one of the largest higher education institutions in Scotland (more than 9,000 students, of whom about 5,600 are engaged in full-time study). The university is named after John Napier (1550–1617), the man who invented logarithms and the decimal point. Napier was born and made his home in Merchiston Castle, a fifteenth-century tower house which, very fittingly, has been conserved and incorporated in the design of the modern buildings on the Merchiston campus.

James Watt Memorial, Riccarton

Heriot-Watt University, Riccarton

THE HIGH STREET

LEGISLATORS, MERCHANTS, LAWYERS AND THE KIRK

*S*INCE the earliest times, the bustling High Street has been the precinct of the legislator, the administrator and the judiciary. Government in all its forms, to say nothing of trade and commerce, was concentrated in this small area. This was the administrative and social nucleus of the ancient burgh. All the levers of power were to be found here, including the influential voice of the Church.

The City Chambers, in which the City Council meets, was built in 1753 as a Royal Exchange to the design of John Adam, the intention being to provide merchants and businessmen with a centre for the conduct of their commercial affairs. In the event, the Royal Exchange was not popular: the businessmen evidently preferred the street, or more congenial premises (such as the taverns). The result was that, in 1811, the Town Council adopted the exchange for its own use.

The rooftops of the Old Town

Castlehill

Euro Summit celebration, 1992

The City Chambers is an excellent example of the architectural surprises that regularly confront the stranger in Edinburgh. Built on a flank of the Old Town ridge, the City Chambers appears on its High Street frontage as a three-storey building; however, when viewed from the rear in Cockburn Street, it is seen to have no fewer than 12 storeys.

The main entrance in the High Street is approached across a quadrangle, the main feature of which is a statue of Alexander of Macedonia taming his famous horse, Bucephalus. The sculpture, by Sir John Steell, originally stood in St Andrew Square but, because of inconvenience to traffic, was moved to its present location. Beneath the archway of the arcade stands the Stone of Remembrance, commemorating those citizens who sacrificed their lives during war service. Immediately within the main doorway of the City Chambers, on panels in letters of gold, is the long roll of lord provosts and their predecessors, beginning with William de Dederyk in 1296.

Across the High Street is St Giles' Cathedral, the High Kirk of Edinburgh, with its distinctive open crown steeple supported by eight flying buttresses. A church has stood on this site since at least AD 854. The present building is basically fifteenth century. Over the centuries it has withstood the shock of war, civil strife and ideological dispute.

The exterior is the unhappy result of an 'improvement' supervised by the architect William Burn in 1829, when the old stonework was refaced. The interior has a more rugged and honest appearance, and includes the beautiful Thistle Chapel (1911) by Sir Robert Lorimer, noted for its ornate wood carving. This is the chapel of the Order of the Thistle, which is one of the oldest orders of chivalry in Europe.

St Giles' also contains memorials to a number of famous Scots, including the

EDINBURGHERS

57

Robert Fergusson

1750–74
POET

•

Fergusson was born in Cap and Feather Close, in the Old Town, his parents having moved to Edinburgh from Aberdeenshire some two years earlier. Robert's health was delicate. At St Andrews University he began writing poetry and it was soon clear he had a gift for satire. He was popular with his fellow students, sensitive, high-spirited and quick-tempered. Returning to Edinburgh in 1768 without a degree, he found a job as a clerk in order to support his widowed mother. In 1772 Fergusson began writing with confidence in the Scots tongue. His poems invoked vivid pictures of life in the Old Town. These were the poems that made his name, and people now spoke of him as the successor to Allan Ramsay.

At the end of 1773, however, acute depression compelled Fergusson to give up his clerking job, and a bad fall some months later led to a deterioration of his mental condition. He was admitted to the public asylum, where he died in October 1774. Robert Burns was to describe the young man as 'my elder brother in misfortune, by far my elder brother in the muse'.

Marquess of Montrose (1612–50) who was hanged at the Mercat Cross a few yards away; and his bitter political rival, the 8th Duke of Argyll (1598–1661), beheaded on the same spot. Also commemorated is a more pacific character, the Edinburgh-born author Robert Louis Stevenson (1850–94).

Parliament Square, at the rear of St Giles', was at one time the churchyard. John Knox, the great Scottish reformer, was interred here, but the exact site of his grave is no longer known. The equestrian statue in the middle of the square is of Charles II ('the Merry Monarch'). The statue, incidentally, is made of lead, and is thought to be the oldest equestrian statue in Britain.

Beneath the arcade is the entrance to Parliament House, once the seat of the Scottish Parliament, which was dissolved on the Union of Parliaments in March 1707. The signing of the Treaty of Union was an event accompanied by great public tumult in Edinburgh, and for many Scots the argument continues to simmer to this day.

Parliament House is now the seat of the supreme law courts of Scotland, for Scotland's separate legal system was retained at the Union. Visitors should see Parliament Hall, a handsome place with an interesting hammer-beam roof that contains not a single nail. The large stained-glass window at the south end, which depicts the inauguration of the Court of Session by King James V in 1532, was made in Munich in 1868.

Café Florentin, St Giles Street

The statues around the walls include one of the novelist Sir Walter Scott, who was a principal clerk of session from 1806 to 1830. Scott, as he sat at the clerk's table below the Bench while wigged counsel droned through some tedious civil case, often must have been turning over in his mind the plot of another historical novel.

Parliament Hall retains a subdued air of activity, thanks to the proximity of the law courts: counsel and solicitors find the great hall a convenient spot in which to confer, obtaining mild exercise at the same time by pacing back and forth at a dignified pace. The Advocates' Library, an indispensable tool of the legal profession, is adjacent.

Also within the building is the Signet Library, whose magnificently decorated Upper Library (1822) by William Stark makes it one of the architectural showpieces of Edinburgh. George IV, on seeing it during his celebrated visit to Edinburgh that year, exclaimed that it was the most beautiful

The Heart of Midlothian was also the site of public executions at one time.

The handsome statue a few yards away is of the 5th Duke of Buccleuch (1806–84), head of a family distinguished in Border and Scottish history.

Immediately to the east of St Giles', opposite the City Chambers, stands the Mercat Cross, which was established about the fourteenth century as a focal point in the official life of the ancient burgh.

St Giles' Cathedral, the High Kirk of Edinburgh

room he had ever seen.

The Heart of Midlothian, a heart-shaped pattern of stones in the roadway a few yards from the main door of St Giles', is a memento of a grim past. For the stones mark the site of the doorway of the Old Tolbooth, the town prison that stood here for some 400 years until it was demolished in 1817. The Old Tolbooth, which was also known as the 'Heart of Midlothian', features in Scott's romantic novel of the same name.

Important public proclamations were made here, business deals conducted, and public executions carried out. The more modern base, incorporating an elevated platform, was a gift to Edinburgh by the statesman and prime minister, William Ewart Gladstone (1885), and royal proclamations are made here on auspicious occasions, with impressive fanfare, by the Lord Lyon King of Arms, attended by members of the Lyon Court.

Old Town architecture

Opposite: Ramsay Garden and the castle

This section of the High Street is rich in interesting closes and wynds that provide knowledgeable locals with convenient short-cuts from the ridge down to Cockburn Street or the Cowgate.

The dramatic views can take the passer-by unawares. For example, at the top of Advocate's Close, framed in the close-mouth is a view of the Firth of Forth, often scattered with distant ships. A century ago, Robert Louis Stevenson put it this way: 'You look down an alley, and see ships tacking for the Baltic.' He may well have had Advocate's Close in his mind's eye when he penned that.

Advocate's Close houses the offices of the Edinburgh Old Town Renewal Trust, and the Old Town Charitable Trust. The Renewal Trust, formed in 1991, has an objective to achieve long-term sustainable improvements in the environment and economy of the Old Town, by promoting a productive balance between the interests of residents, businesses and visitors. The Charitable Trust has been concentrating on the provision of services to homeless people and disadvantaged members of the Old Town community.

Anchor Close, though little of visual interest survives, none the less merits a foot-note in world history as the place where the printer William Smellie published the first edition of the *Encyclopaedia Britannica* (1768) as well as the Edinburgh edition of Robert Burns' poems (1787).

THE PALACE OF HOLYROODHOUSE

"HOLYROOD IS A HOUSE OF MANY
MEMORIES. WARS HAVE BEEN PLOTTED,
DANCING HAS LASTED DEEP INTO
THE NIGHT, MURDER HAS BEEN DONE
IN ITS CHAMBERS...NOW, ALL THESE THINGS
OF CLAY ARE MINGLED WITH THE DUST...
BUT THE STONE PALACE HAS OUTLIVED
THESE CHANGES."

Robert Louis Stevenson. Edinburgh, Picturesque Notes, 1878

THE PALACE OF HOLYROODHOUSE IS HER MAJESTY'S OFFICIAL RESIDENCE IN
SCOTLAND. THE STATE ROOMS AND HISTORIC APARTMENTS ARE OPEN TO
THE PUBLIC THROUGHOUT THE YEAR EXCEPT DURING ROYAL VISITS.
FOR FURTHER INFORMATION CALL 031 556 1096. TICKET OFFICE OPEN
28TH MARCH-31ST OCTOBER, MON-SAT 09.30-17.15; SUN 10.10-16.30.
1ST NOVEMBER-23RD DECEMBER MON-SAT 09.30-16.15; SUN CLOSED.

Mary King's Close, whose rather sinister history is a favourite Edinburgh tale, is unique in the city in that it is now completely sealed from the public street and below ground. The population of the original close was all but wiped out by plague in 1645, and an understandable reluctance by others to move in led to its gradual dereliction. Eventually the close was built over and incorporated into the extended City Chambers.

Conducted tours of this underground close are organised from time to time, and those interested should make enquiry at the City Chambers. It is an eerie experience to explore this deserted, subterranean street, with its flights of worn steps and, at intervals on either hand, a succession of echoing chambers, which once were living homes and shops. The close is said by some to be haunted.

On the south side of the High Street, Old Fishmarket Close offers a particularly steep descent to the Cowgate, from which the pedestrian can scale the far slope to Chambers Street.

Old Assembly Close derives its name from the assemblies (dances), which were a fashionable social entertainment: there was an Old Assembly Hall in the close in the eighteenth century.

No. 180 High Street, the offices of the Edinburgh Festival Fringe Society, could be called the hub of the Fringe: it is here that all information about the annual event may be obtained, as well as tickets for the shows.

A few yards further down the High Street, at its junction with South Bridge, is the Tron Kirk. The name is derived from the salt tron, the public weigh-beam against which this basic commercial product was tested, and which was situated nearby. The Tron Kirk was opened for worship in 1647. During the following three centuries, mainly because of the prominence of its site, the building suffered various vicissitudes

(including the destruction of its spire in the Great Edinburgh Fire of 1824), before it was closed for worship in 1952. The fabric of the empty building, however, was well looked after, and is open in summer as an Old Town Information Centre. Archaeologists have uncovered within the building the cobbled roadway and other interesting vestiges of Marlin's Wynd, which ran from the High Street down to the Cowgate.

St Giles' from the Lawnmarket

Having carefully negotiated the busy junction of the High Street and the Bridges, proceed down the High Street on its north side, keeping an eye open for Paisley Close. It was near here in 1861 that one of the tenements collapsed, a number of the residents being buried in the ruins. As rescuers toiled amid the debris, they were encouraged by a cry, 'Heave awa', chaps, I'm no' deid yet!' The entrance to the close now bears a

64

The Heart of Midlothian outside St Giles'

sculpted likeness of this spirited young man who survived the calamity.

On the same side of the street, Chalmers Close gives access to the Scottish Stone and Brass Rubbing Centre, housed in Trinity College Church Apse. Admission is free. The centre has a fascinating collection of replicas moulded from rare medieval brasses, ancient Pictish stones and other Scottish historical artefacts. Visitors can buy kits with which to make their own rubbings.

No previous experience is required, and staff are on hand to assist.

On the other side of the street is the Museum of Childhood, one of the most popular of the city museums. It was the first of its kind in the world when founded in 1955. The museum was the inspiration of the late Patrick Murray, a town councillor and avid collector, whose personal collection of childhood toys and other memorabilia was soon augmented by a flood of such

Opposite: The Museum of Childhood

gifts as the news spread around the world. To this day, donations continue to be offered to the museum by adults who have no house room but who cannot bear to throw out these souvenirs of their childhood. On five floors there are moving toys, historical slot machines, train sets, musical toys, soldiers, the largest display of dolls anywhere, games – and much more. Incidentally, Patrick Murray, who was a bachelor, always saw his Museum of Childhood as a source of social study, and often claimed that he did not like children!

Across the street again to John Knox's House, which must be the best known of the early town houses in the Old Town. The building, which is known to have been built before 1490, survived into modern times only because of its strong associations with Knox (1505–72), the father of the Scottish Reformation.

The design is typical of houses owned by wealthy citizens at that time: one of the owners was James Mossman, goldsmith to Mary, Queen of Scots. There were many houses like it in the Old Town, but most of them perished, either as a result of fire, deterioration or inevitable changes in living standards. The width of the street at John Knox's House, incidentally, gives a fair indication of the width of the Royal Mile 400 years ago.

Knox, who was minister of St Giles' for about nine years from 1560, is known to have lived in three different manses during his ministry in Edinburgh. Two were fairly near St Giles' and have not survived; this was probably the third. The house is open to the public from Monday to Saturday.

Adjacent is Moubray House, which is thought to be the oldest dwelling in Edinburgh. At the kerb is one of the street wells

EDINBURGHERS

John Knox

1505–72
THEOLOGIAN AND PREACHER

•

The dominant figure of the Protestant Reformation in Scotland, Knox has been roughly handled by posterity, leaving him with a reputation which, some historians argue, is inaccurate and largely undeserved. Knox is associated in the public mind with a narrow bigotry, the promotion of guilt and joylessness, and a philosophy that effectively stunted artistic expression. A more balanced judgment might be that Knox, a powerful preacher and influential leader, has inevitably drawn the blame for the consequences of powerful forces which were abroad in the land and with which Scots by temperament felt an emotional sympathy..

Born near Haddington, East Lothian, Knox was ordained as a Roman Catholic priest but in 1547 joined those Protestant Reformers who had captured St Andrews Castle. When the castle was retaken by the French, Knox was sentenced to the galleys. Released some two years later, he studied in Europe before returning to Scotland, where he became the leading figure of the Reformation.

His tract *Blast of the Trumpet Against the Monstrous Regiment of Women* gave permanent offence to Queen Elizabeth of England and he was a stern opponent of Mary, Queen of Scots.

which provided the Old Town with its first piped supply of water (there are several still to be seen). Men who could be hired to carry pails of water up to the tenement flats were called caddies. The name for these porters survives today on the world's golf courses.

Immediately downhill from John Knox's House is the Netherbow, an arts centre (including a small theatre) run by the Church of Scotland.

Across the street, in Tweeddale Court, the Scottish Poetry Library houses a collection of work by poets in books, cassettes and magazines. A unique facility is its computerised catalogue of 13,000 items, which allows subject searching. Anyone is welcome to visit and use the library. The collection contains works from all periods, from Barbour's 'Brus' to the most recent publications. Gaelic, Scots and English poetry is distributed on loan, and the library periodically has overseas poets in residence

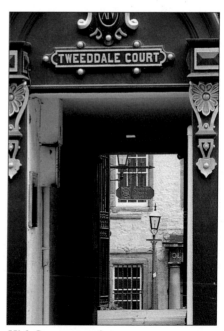

High Street restoration

'Heave awa', chaps . . .'

who give talks in schools, colleges and elsewhere.

We are now approaching the boundary of old Edinburgh, because the Canongate was a separate burgh. The Edinburgh town wall ran here at right angles to the High Street, and at the road junction can be seen brass markers to show the location of the Netherbow Port. This was one of the gates into old Edinburgh, and there is a representation of the gateway inscribed in the wall of the tenement on the north side of the street. Note that the name of the last close on the south side of the street is World's End Close. It must have been named either by an Edinburgh chauvinist or a man with a dry sense of humour. At the other end of St Mary's Street, in the Pleasance, can be seen a surviving section of the Flodden Wall.

John Knox's House, High Street

CANONGATE

THE INDEPENDENT BURGH

*T*HE Canongate, that section of the Royal Mile adjacent to Holyrood Palace, obtained its name from a religious source. In 1128 David I founded a monastery at Holyrood and granted a charter to the adjacent burgh: the thoroughfare of the Canongate was the canons' way, frequented by them as they passed between the monastery (later an Augustinian abbey), the burgh and the castle.

For centuries the burgh of Canongate was quite independent of Edinburgh. Canongate was regarded as a highly desirable place to live: the reason was that, being outwith the confines of the Edinburgh town wall, life was much more spacious. The Canongate was well known for the generous dimensions of its garden ground and its fruit orchards. The presence of the Scottish court at Holyrood naturally attracted the nobility,

Chessel's Court, Canongate

THE ROYAL MILE
A MUSEUM IN ITSELF

1 *T*HE WRITERS' MUSEUM
Treasurehouse of items
relating to Robert Burns,
Sir Walter Scott and
Robert Louis Stevenson

Castle

2

Lawnmarket

1

High Street

*M*USEUM OF CHILDHOOD
Childhood memories
galore - from cuddly
toys to castor oil!

*B*RASS RUBBING CENTRE
Try your hand at
brass rubbing - no
experience needed.

3

2   3

*H*UNTLY HOUSE MUSEUM
Packed with collections
relating to Edinburgh's
past - social history, silver,
glass, pottery, shop signs.

4

Canongate

4   5

5

*T*HE PEOPLE'S STORY
Tells the story of the
ordinary people of
Edinburgh, from the
18th century to the
present day.

Palace

*E*xplore Edinburgh's world-famous Royal Mile where much of Scotland's tumultuous

history was acted out. This is the fascinating setting for five city museums, all within easy

walking distance of each other. But, then, the Royal Mile is a museum in itself.

Open Monday to Saturday, 10am - 6pm
(October to May 10am - 5pm)
During the Edinburgh Festival, Sundays 2pm - 5pm

ADMISSION FREE

many of whom maintained a town house in the Canongate, placing it as near to Holyrood Palace as possible. A number of these interesting dwellings survive today.

Like the Old Town generally, the Canongate sustained a number of social and economic body blows over a lengthy period but especially in the nineteenth century. The result was that large areas were reduced to slums, and it was well into the twentieth century before there was any significant effort in conservation. The impetus for this came from a young architect, the late Robert Hurd, the crucial finance being provided initially by the public-spirited 4th Marquess of Bute. From these modest beginnings, the town itself was encouraged to tread the conservation path. All such work was suspended on the outbreak of the Second World War in 1939, but was resumed in the Canongate in 1952 and progressed steadily thereafter.

Near the top of the Canongate, just a little downhill from Cranston Street, is Morocco Land. It can be identified by a stone figure on the wall, above street level. The figure, thought to be that of a Moor, recalls an Edinburgh legend that the original owner of the building had spent some years in Morocco, possibly as the captive of sea pirates, before he returned to Edinburgh with a Moroccan servant and built this property. There are several variations of the legend, some even more romantic than that related here, and all of them unverifiable.

No. 215 – Shoemakers' Land (1677) – is so named because it was built by the Incorporation of Cordiners (i.e. shoemakers).

There are indeed few buildings in the Canongate that do not have an interesting story attached to them. Across the street is Chessel's Court, seen through an arcade. At the rear of the court is the attractive building which, in 1788, housed the Excise Office that was the scene of the notorious Deacon Brodie's last and ultimately fatal exploit.

The name of Old Playhouse Close commemorates a theatre where, in the eighteenth century, and periodically opposed by the Church and the Town Council, dramatic performances were given. It was here that John Home's *Douglas*, hailed at the time as a milestone in the Scottish theatre, had its première in 1756.

In St John Street can be seen the façade of the house where the Scottish novelist Tobias Smollett (1721–71) lived with his sister in 1766.

Moray House, whose entrance gate is distinguishable by its two slim stone obelisks, was built by the Dowager Countess of Home in 1625. It takes its name from her daughter, who became the Countess of

Silver exhibits, Huntly House Museum

Moray. The property has figured in more than one dramatic episode from Scotland's long story. Oliver Cromwell lodged here on two occasions – the second in 1650 when the parliamentary army entered Edinburgh and Leith following the Scots' disastrous defeat at the Battle of Dunbar.

There is a sinister story attached to the ornate stone balcony that juts out over the street. In 1650, when the Marquess of Montrose, having been captured by the Covenanters, was passing Moray House on the way to his trial, his bitter political rival, the Marquess of Argyll, looked down on him from this balcony. It was the wedding day of Argyll's son, and it is said that members of the wedding party spat on the doomed Montrose from the balcony. The ironies of history! Some ten years later Argyll, his political fortunes transformed, passed beneath the same balcony, en route to his own trial and execution (1661).

Moray House also had a small part in the drama that surrounded the signing of the Treaty of Union in 1707. The commissioners had evidently arranged to meet and append their signatures in the summer house at Moray House. Such was the public tumult raised by those opposed to union with England, that the commissioners were compelled to seek a safer refuge in the cellar of a building in the High Street.

Moray House is now one of Scotland's colleges for the training of teachers, and the original house, though still there, is somewhat overshadowed by educational buildings more modern and less comely.

On the other side of the street is Bible Land, built in 1677 and so called because

Bible Land, Canongate

Moray House

above its entrance is an open book, on the pages of which is inscribed the following verse, inspired by Psalm 133:

Behold how good a thing it is
And how becoming well
Together such as brethren are
In unity to dwell

and, in addition, the message:

It is an honour for men to cease from strife.

in 1570 a new frontage was added, featuring the distinctive triple gable. In 1647 it was acquired by the Incorporation of Hammermen of the Canongate, who extended the building and rented out parts of it. By the nineteenth century Huntly House had fallen on hard times. It was inhabited by the poor, was subject to neglect and decay, and it seemed that the life of the venerable building was nearing its end. However, it was acquired by the City of Edinburgh in 1924

Canongate Tolbooth

Huntly House, which is now the City of Edinburgh museum of local history, is one of the oldest and most interesting buildings in the Royal Mile. It is a fine example of a sixteenth-century town house, and has had a varied career. The property was owned by the Aitchison family from 1517 to 1609. Like many other buildings, it suffered severely when the English sacked Edinburgh in 1544, but rebuilding took place, and then and, after extensive restoration, re-opened as the principal city museum in 1932. Huntly House contains a large and varied collection, illustrating many different aspects of the city's history. There are also outstanding examples of local craftsmanship in silver, pottery and glass. In addition, the museum boasts a personalia collection relating to the First World War leader Field Marshal Earl Haig.

EDINBURGHERS

Allan Ramsay the Elder

1686–1758

POET

•

Originally a wig-maker in Edinburgh, Ramsay gave that up for bookselling. He founded what is thought to have been the first circulating library in Britain. He published his collected poems a few years later. His best known work, *The Gentle Shepherd*, on a pastoral theme, had instant success.

Ramsay is said to have been the most amiable of men and a great conversationalist. Always interested in the theatre, he opened a playhouse in CARRUBBER'S CLOSE, but it was closed down by the Town Council. Ramsay built an octagonal home, the 'Goose-pie', which still stands at RAMSAY GARDEN, Castlehill, near the top of the ROYAL MILE.

Ramsay is buried in GREYFRIARS CHURCHYARD. His marble statue stands at the junction of PRINCES STREET with the MOUND; the medallion portraits around the pedestal are members of his family and descendants.

Bakehouse Close, entered by a typical pend, is a good example of the domestic architecture of the period.

Immediately adjacent is Acheson House (1633), named after Sir Archibald Acheson, who was secretary of state for Scotland in the reign of Charles I. In the 1930s the declining property was rescued by the 4th Marquess of Bute, who in a number of crucial instances such as this championed the cause of conservation and showed the way to others, including local authorities.

The picturesque building with the clock, on the north side of the street, is the Canongate Tolbooth (1591), which was the administrative hub of the Canongate in the days when it was an independent burgh. This was the meeting place of the council, where the law court sat, and the burgh jail. The Tolbooth is now the home of the city's newest museum – The People's Story. This tells of the lives, work and pastimes of Edinburgh citizens from the eighteenth century to the present day. The museum is about those who worked in Edinburgh's industries, trades and services.

Canongate Kirk (1688) is the parish church of the Canongate. As such, its parish includes the Palace of Holyroodhouse, and Her Majesty the Queen and other members of the royal family worship here while in residence at Holyrood. In the churchyard are the graves of many notable Scots, including Lord Provost George Drummond, the man of vision who was the driving force behind the New Town in the eighteenth century; Adam Smith (1723–90), economist and author of *The Wealth of Nations*; the Scottish philosopher, Professor Dugald Stewart (1753–1828); the young poet Robert Fergusson (1750–74), over whose half forgotten grave Robert Burns erected a headstone; Mrs Agnes MacLehose, Robert Burns' friend, 'Clarinda'; and Professor James Gregory (1753–1821), of the Chair of Medicine at Edinburgh who gave a grateful

Opposite: Old College with the Pentland Hills in the background

Canongate Church

Opposite: Back green, Canongate

world Gregory's Powder (a mixture of pulverised rhubarb, ginger and magnesia).

On the north side of the street is a wall plaque marking the site of Golfer's Land. This commemorates a celebrated golfing legend about a shoemaker named John Paterson who about 1679, because of his exceptional skill at the game, was chosen by the Duke of York (later James II) to partner him in a foursome against two English noblemen on Leith Links. The match was won by Paterson and his royal partner, and the story goes that the gratitude of the Duke was so generous that Paterson was able to build the Canongate property with the proceeds.

Whitefoord House, which derives its name from an ancient town house formerly owned by a member of the nobility, is now the title of a complex of buildings that comprises the Scottish Veterans' Residences for ex-servicemen.

The Canongate at this point becomes wider as we approach Abbey Strand and the entrance to Holyrood Palace. Through the arcade and pend on our left lies White Horse Close, a building of picturesque charm, which can be traced back to 1623 but which was extensively restored in the 1960s. This was the spot at which many of the coaches between Edinburgh and London began and ended their journeys. It is thought to have been the inn at which many of Prince Charles Edward Stuart's officers were quartered when his Highland army entered Edinburgh in 1745 prior to the march into England.

The Holyrood Brewery Foundation plans to create a visitor centre which will trace the history of the world on a 10-acre site between Holyrood Road and Holyrood Park.

Abbey Strand was a legal boundary line around Holyrood Abbey, the skeletal remains of which stand immediately north of the palace. Centuries ago, individuals entering the abbey precincts could gain

EDINBURGHERS

Adam Smith

1723–90
ECONOMIST

•

By publishing in 1776 *An Inquiry into the Nature and Causes of the Wealth of Nations*, Adam Smith founded the science of political economy. So significant were the effects of this book for the modern world that it has been described as one of the most important ever written. It is referred to in every history of the subject.

The basic doctrine of *The Wealth of Nations* was that labour is the only source of a nation's wealth. Smith advocated division of labour in the productive process, stressed the importance of individual enterprise and argued the benefits of free trade. The true wealth of a nation, he held, lay not in gold but in the achievement of an abundance of the necessities of life. He warned against unnecessary intervention by the state in this process.

Smith was born in Kirkcaldy, Fife, and his boyhood friends included the Adam brothers, destined to achieve their own fame as architects. As a child, Smith demonstrated an absence of mind which was to be a characteristic throughout his life. He was educated at Glasgow and Oxford, and in 1751 was appointed Professor of Logic at Glasgow University. Eight years later he published his *Theory of Moral Sentiments*, which established his reputation as an author.

The Wealth of Nations, which had been about ten years in the writing, was an immediate success and secured Smith's financial future. In the following year he made his home in PANMURE HOUSE, which still stands in the CANONGATE. There he entertained his friends regularly, including such figures of the Enlightenment as the physicist Joseph Black, James Hutton the geologist, and David Hume.

sanctuary from the civil law, and in consequence quite a community of fugitives developed within the precincts. There was even an arrangement for a kind of amnesty from arrest on the Sabbath and, since the sanctuary took in Holyrood Park and a number of taverns, the confinement could not have been too onerous. The most com-

mon reason for seeking refuge seems to have been financial, for until about a century ago debtors could be imprisoned. The Abbey Strand is still marked in the roadway (with the letter 'S'), but any surviving power the sanctuary may have has not been tested within living memory.

The Stone and Brass Rubbing Centre

Huntly House Museum

White Horse Close, Canongate

HOLYROOD PALACE AND PARK

SCENE OF ROYAL DRAMAS

*T*HE Palace of Holyroodhouse impressively punctuates the end of the Royal Mile. Tall wrought-iron gates of elegant design lead into a spacious forecourt, in the middle of which stands an ornamental fountain of ancient design: it is a copy of a famous one at Linlithgow Palace.

Holyrood, a royal residence which has been the scene of so many dramatic episodes in Scotland's story, was founded by James IV in 1498. However, much of the building that we see today is the result of a reconstruction in 1671 to the orders of Charles II. The palace had been knocked about a bit by the Earl of Hertford in 1544 during his notorious sack of Edinburgh, and then in 1650 some carelessness by Oliver Cromwell's troopers resulted in fire damage.

Holyrood Palace

Opposite: Holyrood Park

Heraldry, Abbey Strand

Abbey Strand

Opposite: Holyrood Palace and Park

Adjacent to the palace stands the ruin of Holyrood Abbey, whose history spans 800 years. A Monastery of Holy Rood was founded here in 1128 by David I, in gratitude for his miraculous escape from an enraged stag while hunting in the Drumshelch Forest. This dense woodland at that time covered a very large area to the south and west of Edinburgh. The incident probably accounts for the fact that the coat-of-arms of the former burgh of Canongate bears a stag's head with a holy cross between the antlers.

Within little more than a decade the monastery had been elevated to an Augustinian abbey. In time the abbey came to play a prominent role in the religious life of a succession of Scottish monarchs. James II, for example, was born there, married there and buried there. He was killed in his thirtieth year when a cannon burst near him during a siege of Roxburgh Castle in 1460. James III and James IV were both married in Holyrood Abbey. James V was crowned there (1524) and buried in the abbey (1542). Within its walls in 1565, Mary, Queen of Scots and Henry Darnley were married. Charles I was crowned in the abbey in 1633.

Like other religious houses of the Roman Catholic Church, the abbey was seriously damaged when the spiritual whirlwind of the Reformation swept Scotland. It was subsequently restored, however, and given a new roof in 1758. Alas, the architects had misjudged the stability of the stone roof, which collapsed ten years later. The venerable thirteenth-century nave was once more a ruin and open to heaven.

Holyrood is the official residence of Her Majesty the Queen in Edinburgh, and is so used when the Queen or other members of the royal family visit the Scottish capital. For that reason the palace may be closed to the public for a number of weeks in summer, but otherwise Holyrood is usually open to visitors.

Fringe Sunday in Holyrood Park

The site of the Sanctuary in Abbey Strand

The very stones of the palace are imbued with the shade of the beautiful, doomed Mary, Queen of Scots (1542–87), who reigned in Scotland for a mere six years but who has left an indelible memory.

What a story! Married at 15 to the Dauphin of France; widowed at 19; returns to her native Scotland and ascends the Scottish throne on a great wave of popularity; marries her weak cousin, Lord Darnley. Her Italian secretary, David Rizzio, is dragged from her presence and stabbed to death. Darnley is murdered in a mysterious explosion and the Queen is suspected of being implicated. Within weeks she marries the Earl of Bothwell. Mary, a devout Roman Catholic, finds her throne assailed by the hurricane of the Protestant Reformation, which has the formidable John Knox at its head. She is humiliated by the mob in the streets of Edinburgh, is imprisoned, persuaded to abdicate, escapes in disguise, is defeated in battle, and flees to England. There she throws herself on the mercy of the English Queen, Elizabeth; is under house arrest for the next 19 years; is then accused of plotting against the English throne, and is beheaded. She was still only 44.

The historian Professor J.M.D. Meiklejohn has described Mary in her youth thus:

> She was already celebrated as the most beautiful woman of her time; and a certain native sweetness and graciousness, heightened by the polish of manner she had gained in the French court, a warmth of affection, gaiety, grace, and generosity combined with her loveliness to form a charm which almost everyone who approached her felt to be irresistible.

It is said that at her death her face retained its exquisite form, but her hair was as white as snow.

It was within the walls of Holyrood that many of the most dramatic events of Mary's life were played out. Visitors may see the

Sunset in Holyrood Park

HM the Queen is offered the city keys

historical apartments, including the spot on which the hapless Rizzio was despatched by a group of ambitious nobles with, it is said, 57 dagger thrusts.

The tour for visitors also includes the more modern apartments of the palace, which have happier associations. These include the long picture gallery, in which royal investitures are regularly held.

The sojourn of Prince Charles Edward Stuart (Bonnie Prince Charlie) at the palace in 1745 was, by all accounts, one of the most glittering events of Edinburgh society in the eighteenth century. After entering Edinburgh at the head of his Highland chiefs, he held court within the old walls, brought the place to brilliant life, and charmed all the ladies in sight, before the candles were extinguished once more. The old palace lapsed back into a long slumber, until George IV made his celebrated visit to Edinburgh in 1822, at the instigation of that universally popular and enthusiastic citizen Sir Walter Scott, who organised the whole programme. George IV, who left an indelible impression on everyone by adopting Highland dress of startling hues, held court in the palace. He was the first monarch to do so at Holyrood for about 170 years.

The General Assembly of the Church of Scotland, the supreme court of the Kirk, is held in Edinburgh in May each year. The Queen does not normally attend in person, instead appointing a Lord High Commissioner to represent her. During the period of the assembly, normally about one week, the Lord High Commissioner resides at the palace and entertains guests there. Afterwards he gives the monarch an account of the debates and decisions taken by the ministers and elders.

Before leaving the palace precincts, have a look at the strange little building known as 'Queen Mary's Bath'. It is thought to be six-teenth century, and its sheer oddity seems to have ensured its survival in an area that

'Queen Mary's Bath'

was otherwise cleared long ago of other structures. A royal bathhouse seems very unlikely. A remnant of the Holyrood Abbey boundary wall, perhaps. Or a royal garden shed? One intriguing story is that during its restoration a dagger was found concealed in the roof: could it have been hurriedly thrust there by one of the fleeing assassins of David Rizzio?

The palace is set against the incomparable backdrop of Holyrood Park, which glorious view from the top, with the whole city, the Forth estuary and the country beyond spread out at one's feet.

A less strenuous and very worthwhile walk within Holyrood Park is to traverse the Radical Road, which runs along the base of Salisbury Crags between the palace and the site of Jeanie Deans's Cottage. The views of the Old Town, with the castle massed high on its rock and hedged about by the city's church spires, are particularly fine. This

Duddingston Loch at dawn

extends to 650 acres and is one of Edinburgh's great blessings. This Royal Park is freely accessible to the public. The walker climbs intriguing hill paths and finds solitude within the space of a few minutes. The highest point in Holyrood Park is Arthur's Seat (822 ft), thought to be a corruption of Archer's Seat. The ascent is not as difficult as it looks. The peak is most easily tackled by way of Dunsapie Loch, and there is a path was a favourite with the present Queen's father, George VI, who enjoyed walking there in the early morning.

Another beauty spot in the park is Duddingston Loch, a reed-fringed bird sanctuary overlooked by Duddingston Kirk. Immediately adjacent is the village of Duddingston, where it is the easiest thing in the world to forget that one is still in a great city, so strong is the rural atmosphere. The

Dunsapie Loch, Holyrood Park

village pub, the Sheep Heid Inn, is one of the oldest in Edinburgh and has an interesting interior. At the other end of the village street, named the Causeway, is a house in which Bonnie Prince Charlie held a council of war immediately prior to the Battle of Prestonpans (1745), when his star was still in the ascendant.

At the gate of Duddingston Kirk is a 'loupin' on stane' (to assist riders to mount their steeds) and a pair of 'jougs' (a set of irons employed at one time for the detention in public of transgressors – for non-attendance at church, perhaps, or for the discouragement of scolding women).

Duddingston

CALTON HILL

A SCATTER OF MONUMENTS

CALTON HILL, though it does not possess the drama of the Castle Rock or the mass of Arthur's Seat, is readily recognisable to the stranger: it's the one with all the monuments scattered about it.

The visitor who climbs Calton Hill and wanders among these impressive memorials dips into a number of chapters of Edinburgh's history. But, first, look at the view. To the west, Princes Street and the castle; to the south, the Old Town with Arthur's Seat crouching in the background; to the east and north lie the Forth, the port of Leith, and our first glimpse of the New Town, of which more later.

The largest of the structures on Calton Hill is the National Monument. It was conceived in 1816 (the year after the Battle of Waterloo) as a memorial to the fallen of the Napoleonic wars. Designed by William Henry Playfair, initially it was to be a reproduction of the Parthenon at Athens. It was

Martyrs' Monument and Governor's House

begun in 1822 but funds ran out. Over the years the fragment has become an accepted part of the Edinburgh skyline, and indeed to many people this truncated war memorial has an appropriate symbolism.

Nearby, the tower resembling an up-turned telescope is the Nelson Monument, commemorating the victor of Trafalgar (1805), which ruined Napoleon's plans for the invasion and subjugation of this country. The monument, built in 1816, has an inte-

and is open to the public.

The small, circular temple commemo-rates the philosopher Professor Dugald Stewart (1753–1828) and was designed by Playfair. The same architect was responsi-ble for the nearby monument to his uncle, the mathematician and natural philosopher John Playfair (1748–1819).

It is not immediately apparent (unless viewed from the south) that Calton Hill was bisected in the early years of the nineteenth

Calton Hill at twilight

rior stairway to the top, where its celebrated time-ball was installed some years later to work in conjunction with the One o'Clock Gun at the castle.

There are two observatories on Calton Hill. The Old Observatory (1792) was designed by James Craig, the architect of the first New Town; and the City Observatory (1818), though superseded by the Royal Observatory on Blackford Hill, remains in use by the Edinburgh Astronomical Society

century by the creation of a broad highway, which was given the name of Regent Road, with Waterloo Place as its approach. Water-loo Place rests upon the Regent Bridge and cuts in two the Old Calton Burying Ground, which as a result now lies behind identical retaining walls on both sides of the street. Within the Old Calton are a number of sig-nificant monuments: these include Robert Adam's memorial to the philosopher David Hume (1711–76); a memorial to Scottish

The National Monument, Calton Hill

David Hume

1711–76

PHILOSOPHER
AND HISTORIAN

•

David Hume, who has been described as the most acute thinker in Britain in the eighteenth century, was born in Edinburgh.

His intellectual powers were recognised with the publication of his *Essays, Moral and Political* in two volumes in 1741 and 1742. Employed as librarian to the Faculty of Advocates in Edinburgh, he wrote a six-volume *History of England* which was extremely popular and admired for its elegant and lucid style. It placed him in the first rank of historians.

In France in 1763, Hume found himself lionised in the salons of Paris, honoured by royalty and regarded as a leading figure of the Scottish Enlightenment.

Good natured, an engaging mix of simplicity and shrewdness, Hume was on friendly terms with virtually everyone. His free-thinking did, however, scandalise some: it is recorded that a devout old woman, having found the corpulent philosopher hopelessly stuck in some deep mud, agreed to extricate the great man only if he recited the Apostles' Creed and the Lord's Prayer.

Hume, who never married, had several homes in Edinburgh, the last of them in what is today St David Street. His tomb is in the Old Calton, Waterloo Place.

soldiers who died in the American Civil War, which is surmounted by a statue of Abraham Lincoln (the first to be erected to the president outside the United States); and a large obelisk, the Martyrs' Monument, which commemorates five political reformers who were transported for sedition in 1793–94.

The imposing building at the western end of Regent Road is St Andrew's House, a part of the Scottish Office. It was completed in 1939, just in time to deal with a mountain of administrative paperwork created by the onset of the Second World War. The building stands on the site of the old municipal prison, the only remaining fragment of which is the Gothic and castellated Governor's House.

In Regent Road, as a magnificent prospect opens out before the onlooker, stands a handsome classical monument to

The Robert Burns Memorial, Regent Road

William Henry Playfair

1789–1857

ARCHITECT

•

More than any other architect, Playfair was the man who earned Edinburgh its label, 'the Athens of the North'. His classical buildings, many on dramatic sites, adorn the city, and lend the physical environment a stature and dignity that is unique in Britain. Playfair was the leading influence in the shaping of Edinburgh's architectural soul.

He was born in London, the son of the architect James Playfair, and as a boy came to live in Edinburgh with an uncle, Professor John Playfair.

On qualifying as an architect, Playfair built a considerable private practice in Edinburgh before designing, in 1820, ROYAL TERRACE, CARLTON TERRACE and REGENT TERRACE, in the New Town. His most important works include the ROYAL SCOTTISH ACADEMY, the NATIONAL GALLERY OF SCOTLAND, NEW COLLEGE AND ASSEMBLY HALL, THE ROYAL COLLEGE OF SURGEONS, DONALDSON'S HOSPITAL, ADVOCATES' LIBRARY and the NATIONAL MONUMENT on Calton Hill. He also enlarged the OLD COLLEGE of Edinburgh University following the death of Robert Adam.

Scotland's bard, Robert Burns (1759–96), who was lionised by Edinburgh society. On the opposite side of the road is the former Royal High School, a classical building (1825–29) designed by Thomas Hamilton, who was inspired by the Temple of Theseus at Athens. In recent years the building has been put to a number of uses, and would probably be the meeting place of a Scottish legislature if such devolution of powers ever came to pass.

Calton Hill also serves as our introduction to the classical architecture that is the hallmark of Edinburgh's Georgian New Town: on a flank of the hill stand the elegant buildings of Regent Terrace, Carlton Terrace and Royal Terrace, all designed by Playfair.

THE FESTIVAL CITY

EDINBURGH GALLERIES AND FESTIVALS

*T*HE City Art Centre, Edinburgh's principal municipal art gallery, is located in a handsome building in Market Street immediately south of Waverley Station. It houses the city's permanent fine-art collection and it is also the venue of a varied programme of temporary exhibitions. It is unique among British art galleries in that visitors are carried to the upper floors by escalator.

The building dates from 1899, when it

served first as a store for newsprint and later as a warehouse for fruit. In 1980, however, having been acquired by the City of Edinburgh, the building was beautifully and carefully converted to its present use.

The city's permanent fine-art collection comprises some 3,000 paintings, drawings, prints and sculptures, mostly by Scottish artists, ranging from the seventeenth century to the present. A.E. Hornel, J.H. Lorimer, J.D. Fergusson, S.J. Peploe, Sir

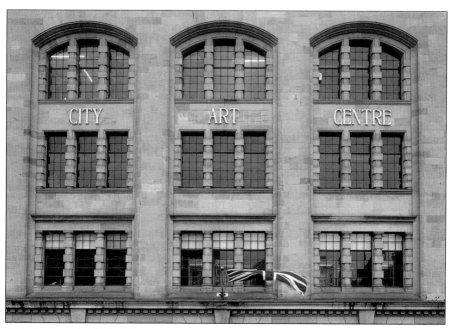

City Art Centre, Market Street

FESTIVAL

EDINBURGH

F E S T I V A L

EDINBURGH

The Scotsman *building, North Bridge*

W.G. Gillies, Anne Redpath, Sir Robin Philipson and Elizabeth Blackadder are among those represented.

Many of the works came as a gift in 1964 from the Scottish Modern Arts Association, or have been purchased with the aid of a bequest made by the late Miss Jean F. Watson.

Many illustrious temporary exhibitions have been held here. Outstanding among these were the Emperor's Warriors, from Xian, China (one of Edinburgh's twin cities), and Gold of the Pharaohs, from Egypt. These two exhibitions attracted a combined total of almost three-quarters of a million people. The attendance at each of them set a record for any exhibition held in the United Kingdom outside London.

The City Art Centre also contains studios for working artists and those working in the crafts, as well as a multi-purpose room for lectures, films and demonstrations. There is a licensed café. The centre enjoys the support of an independent society, the Friends of the City Art Centre and Museums, which exists to promote interest in these institutions. A programme of 'open space' exhibitions offers a venue to local art groups.

Across the street is the Fruitmarket Gallery, an independent gallery subsidised by the Scottish Arts Council and the City of Edinburgh. Its policy is to show a challenging programme of national and international contemporary art, design and architecture. It is also concerned to exhibit the best work of Scottish artists and leading artists from abroad.

Further up the hill, at no. 21 Market Street, are the headquarters of the Edinburgh Festival Society, the body which runs the Edinburgh International Festival of Music and Drama. The Festival, founded in 1947, is held annually during three weeks in August and is now the largest arts festival in the world. The finest musicians, singers,

Opposite: Femme, Le Treport *by John Bellany, City Art Centre*

actors, writers and artists are to be found in Edinburgh at Festival time.

From its earliest years the Festival also attracted to the city more and more amateur and professional groups, who were happy to perform outwith the official Festival, on the fringe of the main event. It was not long before this peripheral activity was formalised as the Edinburgh Festival Fringe Society, and today literally hundreds of shows are presented under its aegis. The range of endeavour on the Fringe is extraordinarily wide and occasionally bizarre. The Fringe is noted for adventure, a ferment of ideas and an irrepressible spirit – a combination that has made an invaluable contribution to arousing public interest in the arts and thus advancing the objectives of the worthy founders of the Festival almost half a century ago. The offices of the Festival Fringe are at no. 180 High Street, a short distance down the hill from St Giles'.

Edinburgh is known far and wide as 'the Festival City'. During the International Festival period there has been since the very first a concurrent International Film Festival. There is also in the course of the year an International TV Festival, an Edinburgh International Jazz Festival, and an Edinburgh International Folk Festival. Now there is an Edinburgh International Science Festival. The festivals proliferate, as more and more people discover that Edinburgh's pleasant environment is an ideal backcloth for any cultural event. Edinburgh is the city that likes to be visited.

Hogmanay, celebrated by Scots on 31 December to mark the passing of the old year, is the oldest of the city's festivals since its origins predate Christianity. So durable and popular is the Hogmanay tradition, bringing large crowds out into the streets at midnight, that in recent years the city authorities have drawn up a programme of festivities for the end of December. The entertainment includes events such as a torchlight procession, street carnivals, concerts, street parties, dancing and fairground fun for all ages.

The city's international links are also fostered regularly through its formal twinning agreements with no fewer than eight other cities – Munich, Florence, Nice, Dunedin, Vancouver, San Diego, Xian and Kiev.

On the corner of Waverley Bridge and Market Street are the offices of the Edinburgh Military Tattoo, which is one of the most stirring spectacles of the Festival. More than 40 years of the Tattoo have proved that there is something thrilling and compelling about performances by military and pipe bands under floodlight, especially when presented against the incomparable backdrop of the illuminated castle. More than 350,000 people from every country in the world see the Tattoo during three weeks of performances on the Castle Esplanade.

Also on Waverley Bridge is an information and ticket centre operated by Lothian Region Transport. Tickets may be purchased here for a wide range of bus excursions, not only in Edinburgh but further afield also. In the same building, the Tattoo public counter sells tickets for the theatre shows in Edinburgh – and also (by computer) for theatres in London, Paris and New York!

In Jeffrey Street is Old St Paul's Episcopal Church, which has an interesting interior. Though the present building is nineteenth century, the congregation's roots run deeper: on this spot stood a wool store which the Episcopalians adopted as their place of worship in 1689, after they had been banished from St Giles' for refusing to acknowledge the sovereignty of William of Orange.

THE NEW TOWN

A CROWNING ARCHITECTURAL ACHIEVEMENT

*T*HE New Town of Edinburgh, which was begun in 1767, is a number of things: it is the site of some of Edinburgh's most majestic architecture, it represents the most significant milestone in the city's history, and it is a distinctive community (some say it is a state of mind!). As Churchill said: 'We make our surroundings, and then they make us.'

Conceived halfway through the eighteenth century, the New Town was born of physical necessity, for the Old Town was overcrowded, malodorous and unhealthy. But the benefits bestowed by the visionary New Town were not only physical, they were intellectual and spiritual also.

Since the Middle Ages and earlier, Edinburgh had been cramped and confined behind its city wall, the cockpit of the Scottish nation, the focal point of constitutional strife, periodically sacked by her powerful neighbour to the south. Not until

St Andrew Square

George Drummond

Robert Louis Stevenson's home, Heriot Row

Opposite: Charlotte Square

well into the eighteenth century was there any true prospect of constitutional stability.

While the social climate for a New Town was ripe, it nevertheless required a great deal of courage and vision on the part of the Town Council, led by Lord Provost George Drummond, to undertake a new town from scratch. Drummond was not a native son, incidentally: he was born in Blairgowrie. The selected site was Bearford's Parks, open land lying immediately to the north of what is today Princes Street Gardens.

It is tempting to imagine a scene (surely it must have occurred at some stage) in which George Drummond stands amid the pasture of Bearford's Parks, on the rough road that led along the ridge, expounding enthusiastically to silent and more cautious companions his dream of a new city on that very spot. No doubt, to some of his fellow councillors, George Drummond was a very alarming fellow.

The birth was preceded by a gestation period of some 15 years. Though proposals were published as early as 1752, it was not until 1767 that Parliament passed the Act extending the boundaries of the town. An architectural competition was won by a young architect, James Craig, with a simple grid design.

The principal street, to be named George Street after the monarch, was to be laid east to west along the gentle ridge of the parks, this thoroughfare being paralleled by Queen Street to the north and Princes Street to the south. At each end of George Street was a square (today St Andrew Square and Charlotte Square). Craig's plan, adopted by the Town Council in 1767, probably won because of the excellent use he made of the site, particularly in relation to the castle, the Old Town and the intervening valley. At the same time, the plan evidently did not see the overwhelming attraction that would be exerted through time by Princes Street, in

EDINBURGHERS

Alexander Graham Bell

1847–1922
INVENTOR

•

The inventor of the telephone was born in a house in South Charlotte Street: there is an inscribed stone beside the doorway. Bell, like his father, was an educator of the deaf. He went first to Canada and then to the United States, where in 1873 he was appointed a professor in the School of Oratory, Boston University.

It was in pursuing his studies on behalf of the deaf that Bell constructed his first rough telephone in Boston in 1875. The instrument that was to revolutionise communications throughout the world was introduced at Philadelphia in 1876 and into Britain and France in the following year.

Bell returned to his native city on visits, and in 1920 was made a freeman of Edinburgh.

combination with the valley, castle and Old Town ridge: Craig was turning his back on the Old Town, with its dark and violent history, and placed his emphasis on the northern prospect, which represented a new and better age.

In the eighteenth century the New Town was a remarkable pioneer venture in town planning, and in the twentieth it remains unique in terms of Georgian architecture. Drummond died in 1766, and so did not live to see his great plan reach glorious fruition. The New Town became his monument. As was said of the aesthetic debt owed by London to the architect, Christopher Wren: 'If you would see his memorial, look about you.'

The first necessity was a good road link across the valley between the Old Town and the New. The North Bridge, begun in 1762, had two purposes: access to the site of the New Town and the provision of a better route to Leith. Craig's New Town materialised from east to west: St Andrew Square came first, construction gradually proceeding westwards. Charlotte Square was not completed until about 1810.

Craig's plan provided for a church at each end, but in the event only Charlotte Square got its church (the handsome domed building that is now West Register House). The blame for this imbalance lies with Sir Laurence Dundas, who had acquired the lease of the land earmarked by Craig for the St Andrew Square church. Dundas proceeded quickly to build what was unquestionably a very fine town house, designed by Sir William Chambers. This handsome house is still there to this day, but it is now the head office of the Royal Bank of Scotland. It is famed for the beauty of the ceiling in its banking hall.

The modern St Andrew Square contains the offices of so many banks and insurance companies that it is said their combined assets make this the richest

Opposite: St Mary's Episcopal Cathedral from the east

square in Europe. The saying emphasises Edinburgh's importance as a financial centre, which in the context of the United Kingdom is second only to London's. The development of the North Sea oil fields, which called for funding on a scale undreamed of in earlier times, gave impetus to Edinburgh's skills in money management.

The column in the centre of the St Andrew Square garden is that of Henry Dundas (1742–1811), the first Viscount Melville, a Tory who was such an influential figure in Scottish political life that in his time he was called 'the uncrowned king of Scotland'.

St Andrew Square also provides access to Edinburgh's bus station, from which services are operated to all parts of Scotland and, indeed, beyond.

George Street contains a great number of handsome buildings, many of them dating from the earliest years of the thoroughfare. As we leave St Andrew Square and proceed west, we see on the right the portico and spire of St Andrew's and St George's Church, which was built here because Sir Laurence Dundas had thwarted the original scheme for St Andrew Square.

Throughout the length of George Street, every cross street presents an interesting prospect – either classical architecture or the castle to the south, or a distant vista of sea and hills to the north. The fact that the land falls away to the north provided the architects of the New Town with an additional dimension to be exploited visually. There are innumerable properties in which the visitor, having passed through an unexceptional entrance, is startled by a panoramic view from the rear windows. He suddenly realises that the back of the building is perched on a cliff.

Between Hanover Street and Frederick

The Royal Bank of Scotland, St Andrew Square

Moray Place

Street are the Assembly Rooms (1787), built originally for the holding of formal dances in gracious surroundings: the elegant rooms are noted for their magnificent chandeliers and numerous wall mirrors. Many a brilliant function has been held within these walls. One of the favourite stories is that it was here in 1827 that Sir Walter Scott finally acknowledged what had been an open secret, namely, that he was the author of the Waverley novels.

The Music Hall was added to the Assembly Rooms at a later stage, and the combined facilities, which are owned by the City of Edinburgh, are regularly used for meetings, concerts, social functions and business conferences. During the Edinburgh Festival they are a principal venue of dramatic and musical entertainment.

In Craig's plan, in addition to the three principal thoroughfares, there was also sensible provision for subsidiary service streets

St John's Episcopal Church, West End

Prince Albert Memorial, Charlotte Square

and mewses. These were later named Rose Street and Thistle Street, and the former has become celebrated in particular as the home of a number of excellent pubs. While it would be invidious to make comparisons on the basis of quality of their product or service, it may be permissible to award the architectural palm to the Abbotsford Bar, which has unsurpassed woodwork, allied to a fine plaster ceiling. Rose Street in recent years has written a new chapter in its history, and one that would not have displeased its eighteenth-century creator: sections of the street are now pedestrian precincts, promenaders strolling among smart boutiques and other interesting shops.

At the western end of Rose Street, on the west side of South Charlotte Street, an inscribed stone records that this was the birthplace, in 1847, of Alexander Graham Bell, the man who invented the telephone and thus changed the world for ever.

And so to Charlotte Square, the north side of which has been described as Robert Adam's masterpiece. The memorial in the centre of the garden commemorates Prince Albert, the husband of Queen Victoria. West Register House, whose noble dome is a prominent landmark of the area, was formerly St George's Church but has now been adapted for a new career as an extension to Register House. No. 6 Charlotte Square is the official residence of the secretary of state for Scotland. No. 7 is the 'Georgian House', and has been furnished by the National Trust for Scotland in order to show the public the lifestyle that would have been enjoyed by a family occupying it in the eighteenth century. Each year many thousands of visitors pass through this magnificent house, which is equipped down to the last iron griddle in its fascinating old-fashioned kitchen. The top floor of no. 7 is the official residence of the Moderator of the General Assembly of the Church of Scotland. Lord Cockburn (1779–1854), Whig lawyer, historian, and

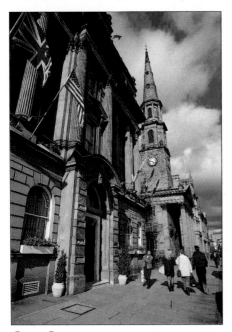

George Street

father-figure of Edinburgh conservationists, lived for a time at no. 14. Field Marshal Earl Haig, the British Army commander in France during the First World War, was born in a house at the south-west corner of the square.

There was more than one New Town: it is a generic title that covers a number of separate developments, executed over a long period for different owners. However, a set of architectural and building controls, adhered to remarkably well in the circumstances, brought about a high degree of uniformity and, as can be seen today, a satisfying homogeneity.

One important factor, which ought not to be overlooked, was the high quality of the sandstone available and the skill of the masons. Both these advantages are now being revealed anew as buildings in the New Town undergo restoration and cleaning.

Queen Street, which was the northern fringe of Craig's New Town, mirrors Princes Street in that it is built up on only one side. This was in order that the residents of Queen Street might have an uninterrupted view of the Firth of Forth and Fife beyond. The well-wooded gardens which run the length of Queen Street are privately owned by the proprietors.

The handsome red sandstone building at the east end is the Royal Museum of Scotland, Queen Street, designed by Sir Rowand Anderson and opened towards the end of the nineteenth century. It contains a comprehensive collection of antiquities illustrating the history of Scotland from the earliest times. The building is shared with the Scottish National Portrait Gallery, whose large collection includes both paintings and rare photographs.

Before the first New Town was complete there was talk of a second. This extended the first from Queen Street

The New Town

Robert Louis Stevenson

1850–94

WRITER

•

The author of *Treasure Island* and *Kidnapped* was born in the Inverleith district, at no. 8 Howard Place, a short distance from the ROYAL BOTANIC GARDEN. When he was about seven the family moved up the hill to no. 17 HERIOT ROW. Stevenson was not a robust child, and throughout his life he never enjoyed full health.

His childhood at Heriot Row inspired in later life many of the charming poems published in *A Child's Garden of Verses* (1885). As a novelist and essayist, Stevenson is admired for his style, imagination and narrative skill. His most popular works are *Travels With a Donkey* (1879), *Treasure Island* (1882), *The Strange Case of Dr Jekyll and Mr Hyde* (1886) and *Kidnapped* (1887).

He travelled widely in Europe and the United States; his wife, Fanny Osborne, was American. In search of better health, Stevenson and his family eventually travelled to the Pacific and settled in Samoa, where he spent the last four years of his life. He is buried there, on Mount Vaea, far from his beloved Pentland Hills.

Gardens northwards, and created streets, crescents and circuses that are now among the most celebrated in Edinburgh. These include Heriot Row, Northumberland Street, Abercromby Place, Drummond Place, Great King Street, India Street and Royal Circus. This second New Town was created over a period of about 20 years from 1802.

Then, to the west, there arose Shandwick Place, Coates Crescent, Atholl Crescent and Melville Street. However, the acknowledged *pièce de résistance* evolved between 1824 and 1827 with the development of the Earl of Moray's property: the preceding developments were brilliantly linked together by the architect, James Gillespie Graham, employing a geometric design that created Moray Place, Ainslie Place and Randolph Crescent.

One of the dominant features of the New Town skyline is St Mary's Episcopal Cathedral, Palmerston Place, with its three towering yet graceful spires. It is seen to best effect from the eastern end of Melville Street. The passer-by will readily accept that this is one of the largest Gothic churches to have been erected in Britain since the Reformation. The money for its construction was bequeathed by two maiden ladies, Misses Barbara and Mary Walker, of Coates, in 1870. The nave was consecrated for services nine years later. The design, by Sir Gilbert Scott, provided a building 260 ft long, and a single spire 276 ft high. The two

Royal Circus

St Mary's Cathedral, Palmerston Place

twin spires were added between 1915 and 1917. Picturesque Easter Coates House, immediately north of the cathedral, is St Mary's Music School.

Stockbridge, another interesting part of the city, has its part in the New Town story. The portrait painter Sir Henry Raeburn, who owned land in the Stockbridge area, feued it out for building in 1813. This led to the creation of such streets as Raeburn Place, Dean Street, the charming Ann Street, India Place and St Bernard's Crescent. There are well-known antique shops in the neighbourhood. Theatre Workshop, whose base is at no. 34 Hamilton Place, is dedicated to promoting theatre in its widest sense, particularly among the young.

Stockbridge lies beside the Water of Leith, and there is easy access to the Water of Leith Walkway. On the walkway between Deanhaugh Street and the Dean Bridge is St Bernard's Well, which has an interesting history. A mineral spring, which had always

St Bernard's Well, Stockbridge

bubbled on the riverbank, was believed by many in the eighteenth century to be beneficial to their health. In 1789 the Court of Session judge Lord Gardenstone, who was convinced the waters eased his rheumatism, commissioned Alexander Nasmyth to build a proper pump-room, surmounted by a Doric temple. At the centre of the pillared temple is a statue of Hygeia, the Greek goddess of health, sculpted by D.W. Stevenson (1888).

The pump-room, which has a fine mosaic ceiling and is beautifully decorated throughout, is open to visitors at certain times. The medicinal waters are not, however, restored.

The Water of Leith Walkway is a series of pleasant footpaths, constructed in recent years along the riverbank. Eventually there will be a continuous walkway throughout the 15 miles' length of the river from its source in the Pentland Hills to its mouth at Leith.

This sketch of Edinburgh's Georgian development is almost complete. However, tribute must be paid to Thomas Telford's Dean Bridge, a graceful masterpiece which soars 100 ft above the Water of Leith to bridge another of Edinburgh's many chasms. Curiously, in view of its public importance in improving access to the north, the Dean Bridge was almost wholly privately funded. Its instigator was Lord Provost John Learmonth, who owned land in the Dean area, north of the Water of Leith, and was

Antique shop, Stockbridge

Dean Village

114

Sir Arthur Conan Doyle

1859–1930
WRITER

•

The creator of Sherlock Holmes was born at no. 11 Picardy Place. He graduated as a doctor at Edinburgh University, where, it is said, the remarkable ability of one of his teachers, Dr Joseph Bell, to make accurate deductions from his observations led Conan Doyle later to create the character of the great detective.

Sherlock Holmes first appeared in a series of short stories in the *Strand Magazine* in 1891. Conan Doyle's talents as a storyteller are also demonstrated in his novels *Micah Clarke* (1887), *The White Company* (1890) and *The Sign of Four* (1890). He served as a physician in the South African War, and in later life became a well-known member of the spiritualist movement.

St Bernard's Crescent

aware that better access was essential if he were ever successfully to feu the land for housing. The Dean Bridge was opened to traffic in 1831 and admirably served its purpose, as such splendid streets as Clarendon Crescent, Learmonth Terrace and Buckingham Terrace eloquently testify.

Almost in the shadow of Telford's bridge is the interesting and picturesque Dean Village, which can be reached by Bell's Brae. The village was founded and

Heriot Row

rural atmosphere only a stone's throw from bustling highways.

An important milestone in the life of the New Town was reached in 1970, with the founding of the Edinburgh New Town Conservation Committee. Funded by the City of Edinburgh, Historic Scotland and the property owners themselves, the committee's continuing task is to conserve the fabric of this cultural asset. This is done by offering grant aid to property owners and

Comely Bank Avenue

prospered in ancient times because its numerous mills derived their power from the river. That economic motivation has gone now, but the village, an architectural curiosity nestling in its tranquil valley only a few minutes from the frenetic roar of the West End, is a convenient and desirable residential area. One of the charms of Edinburgh is that the city continues to nurture a number of peaceful village communities in which there survives a

expert advice on external repairs. The New Town is, of course, primarily a residential area: its hundreds of households form a thriving community and provide the Scottish capital with a living heart. For many years the City of Edinburgh, through its Planning and Development Committee, has actively practised a policy of discouraging the conversion of New Town residential properties to commercial use. The area has been formally recognised by the European

James Clerk Maxwell

1831–79

PHYSICIST

•

James Clerk Maxwell, who was born at no. 14 India Street, Edinburgh, is generally regarded as one of the greatest physicists the world has ever seen. Einstein placed on record his view that the Scot's work resulted in the most profound change in the conception of reality in physics since the time of Newton.

Maxwell's researches united electricity and magnetism into the concept of the electromagnetic field. He died relatively young, and indeed some of the theories he advanced in physics were only conclusively proved long after his death. For example, he did not live to see proved in the laboratory his theory that when a charged particle is accelerated, the radiation produced has the same velocity as that of light: it is a unification that remains one of the greatest landmarks in the whole of science. It paved the way for Einstein's special theory of relativity. Maxwell's ideas also ushered in the other major innovation of twentieth-century physics, the quantum theory.

Community as a valuable part of Europe's heritage: in 1988, the Europa Nostra silver medal was awarded for this 'outstanding example of co-ordinated rehabilitation and maintenance management in an area of high architectural values'. The offices of the New Town Conservation Committee are at 13a Dundas Street, where there is a gallery which presents temporary exhibitions. Admission is free.

LEITH AND NEWHAVEN

EDINBURGH'S DOCKLAND

*L*EITH is, and has been for centuries, Edinburgh's outlet to the sea. Until the coming of modern roads and the railway, the sea was Scotland's commercial highway, and so from earliest times the interests of Edinburgh and Leith intermingled. It is important to remember that, while a degree of control was exercised by Edinburgh, particularly in relation to maritime trade, Leith was an independent burgh until as recently as 1920. Leith has its own long and distinct history, and to this day Leithers retain a strong sense of community.

The visitor will find many clear signs of this maritime tradition, both ancient and modern. The hub of Leith is the bustling intersection known colloquially as 'the Foot o' the Walk'. This refers to the broad highway named Leith Walk, which is the main thoroughfare linking the Port with Edinburgh. It is hard now to imagine Leith Loan (as it was known then) as a country road in

Newhaven Harbour

The Shore

Leith Waterworld

Opposite: Waterfront Wine Bar, Leith

the eighteenth century.

The statue at the Foot of the Walk is that of Queen Victoria. Trinity House (1816), a classical building in the Kirkgate, serves as Leith's maritime museum. Its collection of documents and antiquities may be viewed by arrangement.

Leith Waterworld, a few yards from the Foot of the Walk, is one of the most exciting leisure facilities to be built in the capital for some years. It has been described as the ultimate water experience, for there are more than 20 water features, including waves, geysers, water cannons, bubble beds, a spa, water chutes and a river run for inflatable rides. It has a poolside café and bar, as well as a crèche. One ticket lets you enjoy all the facilities, and there are special offers for groups and party bookings. Every weekday morning local groups take over, including parent and toddler groups, playgroups, and groups for women or disabled people. If you

Sir Eduardo Paolozzi

1924–
SCULPTOR

•

Sir Eduardo Paolozzi was born in Crown Place, Leith, of Italian parents. As a boy he attended Leith Walk School and Holy Cross Academy. He trained at EDINBURGH COLLEGE OF ART, worked in Paris for several years shortly after the end of the Second World War, and then taught in London.

A group of three of his major sculptures, which were commissioned jointly by the City of Edinburgh and businessman Tom Farmer, are on permanent display at Picardy Place.

Sir Eduardo has been Professor of Sculpture at the Akademie der Bildenden Kuenste, Munich, since 1981, and he holds honorary degrees from several universities. He was admitted a member of the Royal Academy in 1979.

He was appointed a Commander of the Order of the British Empire in 1968, and has been Her Majesty's Sculptor-in-Ordinary in Scotland since 1986. He received his knighthood in 1988.

want to arrange a special session or find out about private hire, phone (031) 555 6000.

From the Foot of the Walk, Duke Street leads to the historic open space known as Leith Links. One of the links' more peaceful historical associations is with the early form of golf in the sixteenth century. This was the venue of the famous foursome in the seventeenth century (already described) in which the Duke of York was partnered by an Edinburgh shoemaker. The mounds on the links are thought to be the earthworks dug for Oliver Cromwell's artillery in 1650.

Constitution Street leads from the Foot of the Walk to Bernard Street (where there is a fine statue of Robert Burns) and the Shore. Here the Water of Leith debouches into the Forth. One of the interesting old buildings, the King's Wark, is thought to have stood here since the fifteenth century. Not far away, in Burgess Street, stands picturesque Lamb's House, built in the sixteenth century by a merchant of that name.

Opposite: The Shore, Leith

THE GIFT
OF THE
PRINCE

In the 1930s the building was rescued by the 4th Marquess of Bute and restored. This was the building to which Mary, Queen of Scots was conducted when she landed at Leith from France in 1561. It is now used as a day centre for old people.

Within the extensive and modern Leith Docks are the headquarters of the Forth Ports Authority, administrators of six ports and two oil terminals. The authority is among the top five port authorities in the

Maritime sculpture, Leith

North Junction Street, Leith

United Kingdom in terms of traffic handled. Leith is also a port of call for cruise ships.

Leith has experienced in recent years a boost to its fortunes. The pump was primed by a programme called the Leith Project, funded by public money. Many of the older buildings were restored and cleaned. Landscaping and tree planting led to the improvement of open spaces. The provision of suitable premises encouraged the introduction of fresh commercial activity. The result was a renewed spirit of enterprise in the port, shown for example by a flourishing of interesting restaurants (including fish restaurants) and smart pubs and wine bars. Lothian and Edinburgh Enterprise Ltd (LEEL) continues to work in partnership with the City of Edinburgh and Lothian Regional Council to ensure the area's regeneration. Organisations such as the Scottish Office and Queen Margaret College have plans to move there.

John Crabbie and Co. Ltd, who have been making Crabbie's Green Ginger Wine for some 200 years, welcome visitors to their winery in Great Junction Street at certain times in summer. Crabbie's Green Ginger is still produced to the same handed-down family recipe – raisin wine matured for up to three years, flavoured with cowslips, elder-flowers, cinnamon, cloves, lemons and oranges, blended and fortified with ginger.

Within the James Pringle Woollen

relating the history of tartan.

Coalie Park, at the western end of Great Junction Street, is a pleasant recreational area on the river, created as part of the Leith Project. The park also gives access to the section of the Water of Leith Walkway that leads to Warriston (two kilometres away).

At the western extremity of Leith Docks is Newhaven Harbour, Edinburgh's traditional fish market. Newhaven, still a distinctive community in the seafaring

Dragon boat racing, Leith Docks

Mills, in Bangor Road, there is a Clan Tartan Centre. Its computer archives can trace your clan connection in minutes, and give you details of your clan name, its chief and its tradition. A permanent exhibition shows life as it was in the Highlands, with historical costumes and a video presentation

tradition, can trace its history back to 1504. It was noted for its shipbuilding, and has its place in Scottish history as the birthplace of the *Great Michael* (1511), built on the orders of James IV for the Scottish Navy and described as the biggest and most powerful ship in the world.

NORTH EDINBURGH

THE MOST BEAUTIFUL GARDEN IN EDINBURGH

*M*OST people would agree that the Royal Botanic Garden, in the Inverleith district, is one of the jewels of Edinburgh. It is the city's second most popular visitor attraction after the castle, with nearly one million visitors.

As Scotland's national botanic garden, extending to 72 acres, it contains a plant collection of unique botanical importance. It is administered by a board of trustees and funded by the Scottish Office Agriculture and Fisheries Department. Admission is free.

The garden is widely regarded as one of the finest botanic gardens in the world, with a long and fascinating history. It is an international scientific research institution, with vital research, conservation, public amenity and educational roles.

It has been on its present site since 1820. Its roots, however, go much deeper than that. It is a direct descendant of a physic garden, which was devoted to the

The Royal Botanic Garden: Palm House (1858)

EDINBURGHERS

Sir Harry Lauder

1870–1950
ENTERTAINER

•

Sir Harry Lauder, the popular singer and entertainer, who won international renown, was born in a cottage in PIPE STREET, PORTO-BELLO.

As a boy Lauder worked in a flax-spinning mill in Arbroath, and for a time he was a miner. It was in Arbroath that he first appeared on stage. He had a natural singing voice and a talent for composing simple and tuneful songs.

His stage persona depended heavily on the kilt, a curly walking-stick, and much talk of bawbees and allusions to tight-fistedness, and Lauder's critics complained that he caricatured the Scot. Be that as it may, Lauder was just as popular in his own country as he was in England and innumerable countries overseas.

Songs like *Roaming in the Gloaming* and *Keep Right On to the End of the Road* retain their magic and have become part of Scotland's folk music. He was knighted in 1919, and in 1927 received the Freedom of Edinburgh.

A few years ago, when the new Portobello Bypass was inaugurated, it was named SIR HARRY LAUDER ROAD.

cultivation of medicinal herbs, established near Holyrood Abbey in 1670.

On every day of the year (except 25 December and 1 January), visitors are to be found strolling beneath the trees. The more exotic plants are housed in 11 exhibition plant houses that create climatic conditions ranging from bone-dry desert to the dripping humidity of an equatorial rainforest. There is a very large and internationally renowned rock garden, while the garden's collection of 500 species of rhododendron is also famous.

On leaving the Royal Botanic Garden via Inverleith Row, turn right and within a few moments you will reach no. 8 Howard Place. This was the house in which Robert Louis Stevenson was born. Around the corner from Howard Place, at no. 10 Warriston Crescent, there is a wall tablet commemorating a visit by the Polish composer Frederic Chopin in 1848.

Portobello is Edinburgh's seaside suburb. The name is immutably identified in the mind of every Edinburgher with sand, salty breezes, buckets and spades, squealing children and ice-cream cones. There is a long and wide beach of first-class sand, and a modern indoor swimming pool at Bellfield Street. There is also a nine-hole municipal golf course within the public park.

Portobello Town Hall, at the hub of the High Street, is a handsome building employed for a variety of stage shows, meetings and other events.

Portobello Promenade

TOLLCROSS AND THE WEST END

EDINBURGH'S THEATRELAND

*T*OLLCROSS, a name which evidently derives from a toll-bar that in olden times levied a charge on road users, is one of the liveliest road junctions in Edinburgh outwith the immediate city centre.

Five roads radiate from the familiar landmark of the Tollcross public clock, and the area can claim a reputation as Edinburgh's theatreland. There is the King's Theatre in Leven Street, a handsome Edwardian building with a beautifully conserved interior unsurpassed by any other theatre in the country, and where a varied programme is presented throughout the year. The Royal Lyceum Theatre, in Grindlay Street, also owned by the City of Edinburgh, presents a year-round programme under the aegis of the Royal Lyceum Theatre Company. The Usher Hall, in Lothian Road, is Edinburgh's premier concert hall, seating 2,700, and its platform is graced by the world's finest

The Royal Lyceum Theatre

EDINBURGHERS

Sean Connery

1930–
ACTOR

•

Born and brought up in FOUNTAINBRIDGE, Edinburgh, Sean Connery earned an early wage as a delivery boy on a horse-drawn milk cart. His daily round included FETTES COLLEGE. It is an interesting coincidence that the author Ian Fleming chose Fettes as the school attended by his fictional secret agent, James Bond, a character with whom Connery's name will always be associated.

The actor now makes his home in Spain, but returns regularly to Scotland. He donated the $1,000,000 fee from one of the Bond films in order to found the Scottish International Education Trust, which financially assists individual Scots to develop their talents.

He has honorary degrees from St Andrews University and HERIOT-WATT UNIVERSITY. To promote his native city he made a film, *Sean Connery's Edinburgh*. In 1987 he was awarded an Oscar for his performance in *The Untouchables*.

In 1992 he was made a freeman of his native city of Edinburgh.

orchestras, solo musicians and singers, particularly during the Edinburgh International Festival.

The most recent addition to this impressive roster of the performing arts is the Traverse Theatre, which has made a spectacular leap from a tiny auditorium in the Grassmarket to a brand-new, purpose-built theatre in Cambridge Street, adjacent to the Usher Hall. The theatre was created as part of the Saltire Court office project in Castle Terrace.

The Meadows in autumn

Much new architecture has been sprouting in the neighbourhood. Directly across the street from the Usher Hall is Festival Square, with its ornamental display of water fountains. The sculpture in the square, entitled Woman and Child, commemorates all those who suffered in South Africa during the years of apartheid.

Beyond Festival Square and the

Opposite: Bennet's Bar, Leven Street

USHER'S

TRADE MARK

INDIA

PALE ALE

EDINBURGHERS

Elsie Inglis

1864–1917
MEDICAL PIONEER

•

Elsie Inglis was a pioneer in a number of ways – most of them associated with the study and practice of medicine. Born in India, she studied medicine at Edinburgh, Glasgow and Dublin, became a general practitioner in Edinburgh, and in 1901 inaugurated a maternity hospice, staffed entirely by women, at EDINBURGH BRUNTSFIELD HOSPITAL.

In 1906 Elsie Inglis founded the Scottish Women's Suffrage Federation, from which sprang, at the outbreak of the First World War in 1914, the organisation of Scottish Women's Hospitals. In the following year she joined this organisation's Serbian unit, and worked in the war-torn Balkans. In a particularly famous episode, she and her colleagues remained at their posts at Krushevac in the face of a German invasion of the area. She also served in Russia and Rumania, and her humanitarian work was remembered with gratitude long afterwards in the Balkans.

In Edinburgh her name was commemorated for many years in one of the city's maternity hospitals, but the Elsie Inglis Hospital is now closed.

Sheraton Hotel is rising the Edinburgh International Conference Centre (described on page 170), due to be completed in 1995. This long-needed facility will give renewed impetus to conference business in Edinburgh – a city which has always been an attractive venue to conference organisers.

A few yards south of Festival Square, at no. 88 Lothian Road, is Filmhouse, the headquarters of the annual Edinburgh International Film Festival. Within Film-

The Meadows in summer

house are the offices of Edinburgh Film Guild, which is the world's oldest film society. A wall plaque beside Filmhouse records that the adjacent building was the birthplace and family home of the actor and director Alastair Sim.

The Meadows and Bruntsfield Links, lying on either side of Melville Drive, are the biggest recreational space in this part of the city. The Meadows, a large stretch of

The Meadows in spring

The Golf Tavern

Muriel Spark

1918–

WRITER

•

Muriel Spark was already well known for her critical studies and verse before embarking on the novels that have established her reputation as one of this country's most respected writers.

She was born in Edinburgh and educated at James Gillespie's School for Girls and Heriot-Watt College. During the Second World War she was employed in the Foreign Office Political Intelligence Department.

In 1954 Muriel Spark was converted to Roman Catholicism, and three years later published *The Comforters*, whose religious theme was dealt with satirically. Her next novel, *The Bachelors* (1960), was about spiritualism, while *The Ballad of Peckham Rye* (1960) imagined the manifestation of satanism in a prosaic suburb.

Her most well-known work, certainly in her native city, is probably *The Prime of Miss Jean Brodie* (1961), a witty portrait of a highly individual and influential teacher at an Edinburgh girls' school between the wars.

She was appointed OBE in 1967 and has been awarded the honorary degree of Doctor of Letters by the University of Strathclyde (1971) and the University of Edinburgh (1989).

wooded parkland criss-crossed with paths, is used by large numbers for football, cricket, hockey, tennis, bowls and jogging. At one time it was a large sheet of water called the South Loch or Burgh Loch, and centuries ago it provided the town of Edinburgh to the north with its main water supply. Local breweries benefited from the water, too. Drainage of the loch, however, was completed by about 1740 and the Meadows were laid out more or less in the form seen today.

The Jawbone Arch in Melville Drive, near to its junction with Marchmont Road, originally came from Shetland, a whaling area at that time, in order to be exhibited at an International Exhibition held on the Meadows in 1886. The tall ornamental pillars at each end of Melville Drive were erected to celebrate the same occasion.

Bruntsfield Links, which extends to about 35 acres, is the last remnant of the historic Burgh Muir, which once stretched southwards from here as far as Blackford Hill and Morningside. A mixture of grazing land, gorse and woodland, the Burgh Muir was given to the city by James IV under a charter of 1508. On at least six occasions the Burgh Muir was the gathering point of a Scottish army: the most fateful of these occasions was in August 1513, when the army under James IV set off for the disastrous Battle of Flodden.

The links also has long associations with the game of golf: indeed, Bruntsfield Links has a claim to be one of the cradles of the game in Scotland. Though in time a lack of space led to the links being supplanted in popularity by Musselburgh and by the Braid Hills (as better roads and transport enabled golfers to travel further afield), there seems no doubt that golf was played on the Burgh Muir as early as anywhere else in Scotland. The Golf Tavern, which is situated only a few yards from the first tee, claims to have been established in 1456.

THE SOUTH SIDE

IN THE SHADOW OF THE CRAGS

*T*HE brilliant qualities of the emergent New Town, north of Princes Street, should not blind us to what was happening during the same period to the south. The 'South Side' (as it is still known with affection) was a name already coined at a time when the Town Council remained to be persuaded in 1767 to take its courage in both hands and proceed with James Craig's plan for the north side.

Immediately to the south of the town, such streets as Bristo Street, Nicolson Street and George Square were all taking shape during the 1760s. People of rank, learning and wealth were taking up residence in this area, in preference to the malodorous and overcrowded Old Town. The family of Walter Scott (his father was a Writer to the Signet) moved to no. 25 George Square in 1771 when Scott was an infant. George Square was Scott's home, on and off, for 26 years.

South Side skyline

EDINBURGHERS

Dorothy Dunnett

1923–

WRITER AND PAINTER

•

Dorothy Dunnett, best known to the public for her skilful and closely researched historical romances, was a professional portrait painter and sculptor long before she was a writer.

Born in Dunfermline, Dorothy Dunnett was educated at James Gillespie's High School, Edinburgh; Edinburgh College of Art; and Glasgow School of Art. Her home has been in Edinburgh for many years.

As a young woman she was a civil servant. She became a professional portrait painter in 1950.

It was only in the 1960s that she turned to writing. Her first novel, *Game of Kings*, was published in 1962. This was a historical romance set in sixteenth-century Scotland, in which the central figure is a fictional Scottish mercenary soldier, Francis Crawford of Lymond. During the ensuing decade, this popular romance developed into a cycle of six novels.

Dorothy Dunnett has also written a second historical series, of which the first was *Niccolo Rising* (1986) about a group of fifteenth-century merchant traders.

The snag about settling in the South Side was that these fine new properties lay outside the royalty, and therefore were beyond the jurisdiction of the Town Council. That meant they lacked good access from the town: to reach the new South Side meant descending into the Cowgate and then climbing the opposite slope. A bridge to span the Cowgate was mooted as early as 1775, but the South Bridge did not materialise until 1788. It is interesting that by that time, a number of residents of the New Town were thinking of acquiring second homes – and were looking for a 'country house' in the rural surroundings of the South Side! The South Bridge, when it did take shape, was very substantial: it had 19 arches and was more than 1,000 ft long. The shops and houses constructed along each side of it proved extremely popular.

Today it is easy to pass along this busy street without being aware that one is crossing a long and high bridge: the situation is revealed only as the pedestrian reaches a gap and sees the Cowgate far below.

The Edinburgh Festival Theatre in Nicolson Street is the city's most exciting development in the performing arts for many years. The Festival Theatre is being created by extending the beautiful Empire Theatre (designed by W. and T.R. Milburn in 1928) to equip it with the largest stage of any presenting theatre in Britain. It will be able to accommodate the world's largest opera, dance and musical companies as well as present drama and variety. There is also a cabaret stage and room for changing exhibitions of art. The width and height of the proscenium will show ballet, dance and opera to the best effect. Many important features of the original auditorium, including the mahogany fittings, are retained, and the orchestra pit can accommodate up to 120 players. It is Scotland's first major lyric theatre.

Opposite: Parkside Terrace

The Festival Theatre, Nicolson Street

It is difficult now to visualise this historic area of the city as it once was, but Lord Cockburn, in his *Memorials*, has left us a fascinating glimpse. Recalling his boyhood (he was born in 1779) at the family home at Hope Park, at the eastern end of the Meadows, Cockburn wrote:

> . . . nearly the whole country to the south of us, though all private property, was almost quite open. There were few fences south of the Meadows. The lands of Grange, Canaan, Blackford, Braid, Mortonhall and many other now enclosed properties, were all . . . unenclosed; and we roamed at pleasure till we reached the Pentlands, or the deserts of Peeblesshire. A delightful region for wild active boys.

At that time, a remnant of what had been the convent of St Catherine of Siena (founded in 1517) still stood in a field behind the Cockburn home. The convent gave its name to the Sciennes district, and the lands of which Cockburn spoke so fondly are now noted for their villas, quiet streets and secluded gardens behind long stone walls. The semi-rural atmosphere survives.

In Dalkeith Road are the Pollock Halls, Edinburgh University halls of residence that occupy a delightful site on the border of Holyrood Park and Prestonfield Golf Club. In the university vacation, the halls are available to accommodate parties from out of town, including those attending conferences in the city.

The leading concert hall on this side of the city is the Queen's Hall, in Clerk Street, at which a wide variety of cultural events is presented throughout the year.

The Jewish community in Edinburgh have long associations with the Newington district, and their synagogue is at no. 4 Salisbury Road. The Islamic community's central mosque is in Potterrow.

TO THE PENTLANDS

TOWARDS STEVENSON COUNTRY

THE road that passes through the residential areas of Bruntsfield, Churchhill and Morningside, known long ago as the Old Biggar Road, is still one of the main exits from Edinburgh for those bound for the south or south-west. Churchhill is another of those dramatic summits that are encountered everywhere by the traveller in Edinburgh. The handsome red sandstone building at the crest of the hill is the Churchhill Theatre. One of the city's municipal theatres, it was converted in 1965 from the premises of Morningside Free Church and is used mainly by the many amateur companies in Edinburgh.

At this point the road plunges dramatically down into the heart of Morningside, which once was a country village lying far outside Edinburgh. The origin of its pleasant name remains a mystery.

Against the wall outside the former Morningside Parish Church (a building now

Swanston Village

belonging to Napier University) stands the reputed Borestone. It is said to have been the traditional rallying point on the Burgh Muir when Scottish monarchs sent out a call for the assembling of the army. From this spot, near the top of Churchhill, there is a rewarding glimpse of the Pentland Hills, whose ridge forms the very boundary of modern Edinburgh.

Beyond Morningside Station the land begins to rise gradually again towards

Marchmont architecture

the Braid Hills and Fairmilehead. Now the country is opening up and the view of the Pentlands becomes increasingly dramatic. To our left are the Braid Hills, acquired by the City of Edinburgh in 1889 and now the site of two outstandingly scenic municipal golf courses. Immediately to the north of the Braids, in the valley of the Braid Burn, is the well-wooded public park known as the Hermitage of Braid. Adjacent to the Hermitage is Blackford Hill, a great fav-

The Hermitage of Braid

south to Hillend Park, with its spectacular artificial ski-slope. The skiers' chairlift is also used by many hill walkers as a useful way to reach the northern ridge of the Pentland range, where there are a number of footpaths offering easy walking and air like wine. The Pentland Hills stretch to the south-west for some 15 miles, and are traversed by signposted footpaths at several points.

Here we are in Robert Louis Stevenson

Royal Observatory, Blackford Hill

ourite with strollers, which is surmounted by the Royal Observatory (1895), where there is a visitor centre.

Fairmilehead is an important crossroads. Westwards the road leads to Oxgangs, the picturesque village of Colinton in its dell, and Craiglockhart.

A short distance south of Fairmilehead crossroads is an access to the Edinburgh City Bypass, but we continue a little further

country, for his summer home was in the hamlet of Swanston, half-concealed among the trees in the shadow of the hill called Caerketton. Stevenson loved the view of Edinburgh from here:

> From the summit, you look over a great expanse of champaign sloping to the sea . . . So you sit, like Jupiter on Olympus, and look down from afar upon men's life.

Hillend Ski Centre

The Pentlands were also a favourite haunt of Lord Cockburn, whose last home was Bonaly Tower, not far distant. He wrote: 'Unless some avenging angel shall expel me, I shall never leave that paradise.' He also said:

> There is not a recess in the valleys of the Pentlands, nor an eminence on their summits, that is not familiar to my solitude. One summer I read every word of Tacitus in the sheltered crevice of a rock (called 'my Seat') about 800 ft above the level of the sea, with the most magnificent of scenes stretched before me.

CORSTORPHINE

HOME OF A GREAT ZOO

*C*ORSTORPHINE is the home of Edinburgh Zoo. Founded by the Royal Zoological Society of Scotland in 1913, the zoo has more than 1,500 animals – by far the largest collection in Scotland – and is open to the public 365 days of the year. The entrance, in Corstorphine Road, is just over two miles from the city centre.

The zoo is beautifully situated in 80 acres of parkland on the slopes of Corstorphine Hill, and offers unrivalled views of the surrounding countryside.

There is a famous and very popular colony of penguins – gentoos, kings, macaronis and rockhoppers – which is the largest in Europe. They live in the biggest penguin enclosure to be found anywhere in the world. A suspension bridge gives visitors a superb aerial view of the penguin pool, while glass panels in the side of the pool also allow underwater viewing. Each afternoon in summer the penguins parade outside

Edinburgh Zoo, Corstorphine

their enclosure, mingling with the public.

The zoo co-operates with other zoos abroad in the breeding of endangered species, and has an education department which runs guided tours on this aspect of its work, programmes for schools and animal-handling classes.

The principal art gallery in this part of the city is the Scottish National Gallery of Modern Art, in Belford Road. The gallery, housed in a classical building in its own grounds, has a collection that is representative of many of the most important modern masters, including Picasso, Matisse and Moore. There is also a fine collection of the best work of twentieth-century Scottish artists.

In the Car, *by Roy Lichtenstein, Scottish National Gallery of Modern Art*

QUEENSFERRY AND CRAMOND

ON THE SHORE OF THE FORTH

*Q*UEENSFERRY, an attractive and historic town on the south shore of the Firth of Forth, stands between the two spectacular bridges that span the Forth. Both structures are among the largest bridges in the world.

The Forth Railway Bridge, opened in March 1890, was eight years in the building and contains almost 54,000 tons of steel. At the time it was the biggest bridge in the world and the sheer scale of its cantilever design immediately made it the engineering wonder of the age. When Sir William Arrol, the engineer who built it, was asked how long it would last, he replied: 'For ever – if you look after it.' For that reason, painters have been continuously at work on the bridge ever since: when they reach the end, it is time to begin over again. A special paint was created for the Forth Bridge by a Leith firm, which has supplied it since 1890.

The Forth Road Bridge, which opened

The Forth Bridge

This beautiful Edwardian Theatre hosts the best of touring drama and entertainment. The theatre's current programme includes West End musicals, a season of top quality drama, two visits by the Royal Shakespeare Company and popular children's shows. If yours is a Winter visit, don't miss the traditional Scottish pantomime.

The KING'S is situated in Tollcross, surrounded by many of Edinburgh's best restaurants, is well served by regular buses and within easy walking distance of the city centre.

Edinburgh's elegant Assembly Rooms is centrally located in George Street and provides the venue for a wide range of events: from ceilidhs and world music concerts to antique fairs and art exhibitions.

The Assembly Rooms is a popular venue offering excellent catering and staging facilities.

Edinburgh's premier concert hall presents musical events for all tastes throughout the year. Rock, pop and country music concerts are a regular feature of a programme that also includes visits by the world's top orchestras.

Closer to home, the Royal Scottish National Orchestra and Scottish Chamber Orchestra provide weekly concerts for much of the year. The Usher Hall is a short walk up Lothian Road from the west end of Princes Street.

Visit the Ticketline ticket shop at the **Assembly Rooms** for information on all events in the city and tickets for most of them, or dial the following numbers ....

TICKETLINE: 031 - 220 4349 for theatre and concert tickets.

The HOTLINE: 031 - 228 9428 for inclusion on our mailing list.

Hiring and conferencing facility information: 031 - 228 8616 .

in September 1964, is a suspension bridge and offers an interesting architectural contrast with its more massive neighbour. It is one-and-a-half miles long – slightly shorter than the rail bridge. The main towers are 500 ft high, and the central span between the towers is 3,300 ft long.

Both bridges emphasise the historical importance of the Forth crossing: the opening of the Forth Road Bridge finally brought to an end a ferry service that could be traced

The Burry Man

Queensferry and the Forth Road Bridge

back 800 years.

The Forth crossing came to prominence in the reign of Malcolm III, known as Malcolm Canmore, whose court was at Dunfermline in Fife and who required a ferry regularly to travel to and from Edinburgh. His Queen, Margaret, a Saxon princess, was a saintly woman who is credited with a civilising influence on the rough Scottish court. She performed many good works among the people, who revered her. It is Margaret who is commemorated in the name of Queensferry, and her likeness appears on the burgh's coat-of-arms.

EDINBURGH SUBURBS

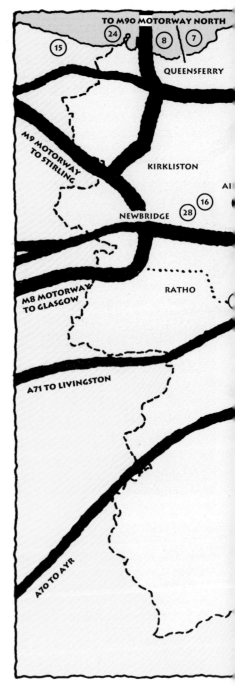

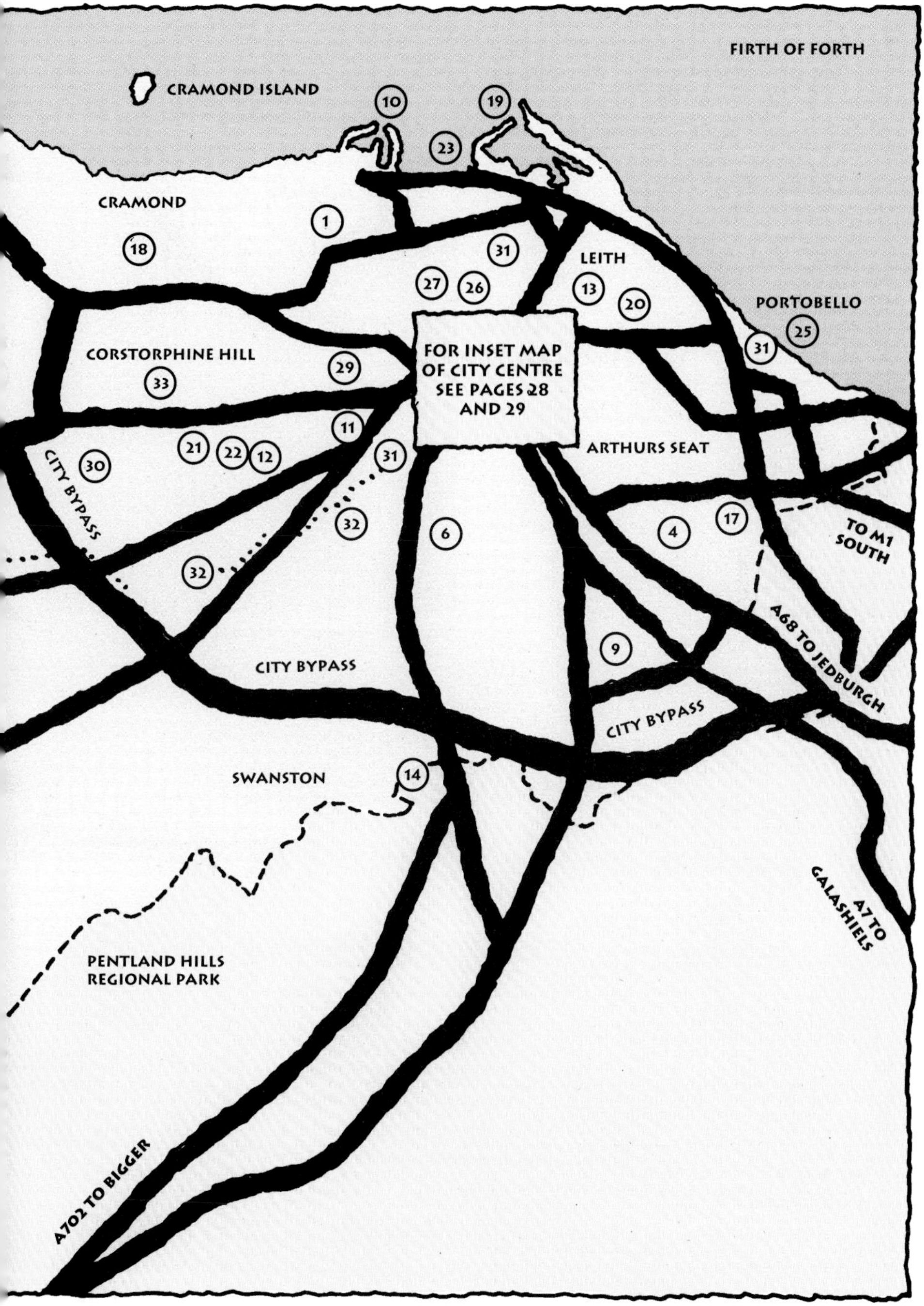

FIRTH OF FORTH

CRAMOND ISLAND

⑩ ⑲
㉓

CRAMOND

①

⑱

⑪

LEITH

㉗ ㉖ ⑬ ⑳

PORTOBELLO

CORSTORPHINE HILL

㉙

FOR INSET MAP
OF CITY CENTRE
SEE PAGES 28
AND 29

㉕

㉝

③①

⑪

㉚ ㉑ ㉒ ⑫

③①

ARTHURS SEAT

CITY BYPASS

㉜

㉜

⑥

④ ⑰

TO M1
SOUTH

A68 TO JEDBURGH

⑨

CITY BYPASS

CITY BYPASS

SWANSTON

⑭

A7 TO GALASHIELS

PENTLAND HILLS
REGIONAL PARK

A702 TO BIGGER

The Queensferry Museum, which is housed in the Burgh Chambers, has exhibits reflecting the life and work of Queensferry down the centuries, including its local industries and crafts. One of the most unusual items in the museum is a life-size model of the 'Burry Man', a weird figure who represents a tradition far older than anything else the visitor will encounter in Queensferry. The Burry Man appears in the streets of Queensferry once a year, during the annual Ferry Fair in August. He is clothed from head to foot in a special suit, to which burrs have been attached by the hundred (burrs are the spiky seedcases of the burdock plant). The custom is so old that no one knows its origin or purpose, but it is thought to relate to a pagan ritual invoking good fortune for the community – perhaps for a good harvest. The whole town turns out to watch the Burry Man's progress through the town.

Dalmeny House, Queensferry

Hopetoun House, Queensferry

Hawes Inn, Queensferry

During the summer there are regular sailings in the *Maid of the Forth* to Inchcolm Island, departing from Hawes Pier. Inchcolm has a twelfth-century Augustinian abbey, now under the care of a resident custodian. Part of the island is a bird sanctuary, and the waters surrounding it abound with grey seals. There are also evening cruises on the Forth, with a shipboard jazz band, to view the spectacularly floodlit Forth Bridge.

Opposite the Hawes Pier is the historic Hawes Inn, a former coaching inn described in Sir Walter Scott's novel, *The Antiquary*. The inn also intrigued Robert Louis Stevenson, who featured it in his novel, *Kidnapped*.

There are two stately homes in the vicinity that can be visited. Dalmeny House, the home of the 7th Earl and Countess of Rosebery, was designed in 1815, and the architectural interest ranges from the Gothic splendour of the hammer-beamed hall to fan-vaulted corridors and the classical

LAURISTON CASTLE

AN EDWARDIAN HOME

A late 16th century tower-house with 19th century additions, Lauriston Castle is situated only three miles from the centre of Edinburgh and stands in attractive grounds overlooking the Firth of Forth. The house's principal apartments have remained unchanged for over sixty years and contain a rich collection of decorative art.

Today visitors are given a unique glimpse of Edwardian life in a Scottish country house.

Open April - October : 11am - 1pm, 2pm - 5pm daily (except Friday).
November - March : 2pm - 4pm Saturday and Sunday only.

Visitors are taken on a guided tour lasting approximately 40 minutes (last tour leaves 40 minutes before closing).

Admission £2 or £1 for concessions. Free car park.
Free admission to grounds. Party visits by prior application.

For more information, telephone 031 336 2060.

Bus no 41 from George Street to Castle gates / No 40 from the Mound to Davidsons Mains.

Old Cramond Brig

design of the main rooms. Within the house is a splendid array of paintings, furniture, tapestries, porcelain and other works of art from the Rosebery and Rothschild collections. The Napoleon Room contains paintings of the emperor, furniture used by him, and the Duke of Wellington's campaign chair.

The other stately home in the neighbourhood is Hopetoun House, the home of the 4th Marquess of Linlithgow. It has been described as Scotland's greatest Adam mansion. Set in a hundred acres of parkland, Hopetoun House has been the home of the Hope family ever since it was built in the early eighteenth century. Much of the original furniture and hangings made for these rooms survive today, and the family's art collection includes many works by famous painters. In the grounds there is a nature trail, herds of fallow deer and red deer, and a flock of rare St Kilda sheep (which are black and have four horns). There is a very pleasant walk of four-and-a-half miles through the Dalmeny Estate, with views of the Firth of Forth, between Queensferry and Cramond. At the Cramond end, there is a ferry across the River Almond (daily except Friday).

Cramond is an attractive suburb of Edinburgh, celebrated for its community of whitewashed houses situated on a slope leading down to the River Almond.

Cramond has a significant place in the history of the area, for this was the spot

Cramond Kirk

where the Romans, in the second century AD, established a port from which to supply their garrisons on this most northern frontier of the Empire. The foundations of their fort are still to be seen in the tree-shaded grounds of Cramond Parish Church; and some 20 years ago, the substantial remains of a Roman official's mansion were uncovered by chance in the middle of the village during excavations for a carpark.

Another of Edinburgh's fine municipal

Lauriston Castle

golf courses is a short distance away at Silverknowes, and the municipal caravan and camping park is situated in the same area. The caravan park is beautifully situated in parkland overlooking the Firth of Forth and has excellent amenities.

Lauriston Castle, standing in pleasant grounds off Cramond Road South, has an interesting history and is well worth a visit. Its last owner, Mr William Reid, was a cabinetmaker and collector, and he and his wife bequeathed the property and its contents to the nation. Since the death of Mrs Reid in 1926, Lauriston Castle has been administered by the City of Edinburgh under trust.

To tour the castle is to step back in time, for a condition of the Reid bequest was that the property should be maintained much as it was in their lifetime. This is a country mansion redolent of the Edwardian era, beautifully furnished, and possessing that air of tranquillity and order essential to gracious living. This atmosphere extends to the grounds, with their trim lawns and mature trees, overlooking the waters of the Forth.

Lauriston Castle has had more than one famous owner. The oldest part is the tower house at the south-west corner, built about 1590 by Sir Archibald Napier, who was the father of the even more celebrated mathematician and inventor of logarithms (for more about him, see Napier University on page 54).

The River Almond at Cramond

A later owner was John Law (1671–1729), who emigrated to France and made his career there so successfully that he was appointed what would be termed today chancellor of the exchequer. He is credited with having introduced paper money to France. Alas, the ambitious Scot was subsequently brought to financial ruin by his business interests.

The extension to the original sixteenth-century tower was built in 1827 by Thomas Allan, banker and newspaper proprietor; this addition, in the Jacobean style, is by William Burn. A library was added later in the same century. Lauriston Castle was acquired by Mr and Mrs Reid in 1902.

Another interesting open space in this vicinity is Cammo Estate, which is administered by the City of Edinburgh as a wilderness park. Conducted walks are organised periodically to study the local flora and fauna.

153

Main Street, Cramond

Port Edgar, Queensferry

The Barnton area is also the home of two of Edinburgh's oldest and most distinguished golf clubs, the Royal Burgess and the Bruntsfield. Both clubs were founded in the eighteenth century, and both began their life on the historic Bruntsfield Links on the other side of Edinburgh. In the 1870s both clubs moved to Musselburgh and remained there for two decades before settling in their present homes at Barnton – the Royal Burgess in 1894 and the Bruntsfield one year later.

In the open country to the west is Edinburgh International Airport, conveniently placed only eight miles from the city centre. A regular bus service is available from Waverley Bridge.

Queensferry

Queensferry High Street

WEST EDINBURGH

EDINBURGH'S RURAL FRINGE

*T*HE western edge of Edinburgh is the most rural part of the city, and in many ways the most charming. Yet it is unknown territory to many lifelong Edinburgh dwellers. People who can reel off the names of every street between Bruntsfield and Stockbridge become hesitant about the terrain between Ratho and Kirkliston. Yet Edinburgh's rural hinterland is very accessible. Indeed, the sudden transition from city to country can be startling. In Sighthill, for example, the motorist one moment is driving westwards past high-rise flats; the next, the urban scene has abruptly vanished and he is among green fields, hedgerows and grazing cows. No conjuror could do it more smoothly.

In this well-cared-for landscape, such village communities as Kirkliston, Ratho and Balerno sit comfortably in their rural environment. Truly, this is where the town meets the country. The Union Canal passes

Bridge Inn, Ratho, by the Union Canal

through Ratho, and cruises on the canal aboard the *Pride of the Union* depart from the Bridge Inn. These cruises operate throughout the year, and there is a restaurant and music on board.

There are well-known golf courses at Ratho Park and at Dalmahoy. A short distance to the south the Water of Leith, having risen in the Pentland Hills, is passing through Balerno, Currie, Juniper Green and Colinton on its way to the city and the sea.

Royal Highland and Agricultural Show

All these villages once owed their prosperity to this river, which turned the water mills that drove the modest industries established on its banks. Though all these villages have grown greatly in the past half-century, each still retains an older architectural core that offers the discerning passer-by a glimpse of an earlier era.

Colinton, where the river passes through a precipitous dell, is one of Edinburgh's most picturesque villages.

Robert Louis Stevenson knew Colinton well, having spent many happy childhood hours at Colinton manse, where his grandfather was parish minister. Nowadays the river is accompanied on its course by the pleasant Water of Leith Walkway, which provides walkers with a leafy, traffic-free route for some 15 miles from high moorland to seashore. Currie and Balerno both provide access to the Pentland Hills, whose footpaths are well signposted.

At Ingliston is the Royal Highland Showground, home of Scotland's premier agricultural show in June each year. Ingliston also has a large exhibition hall and facilities for the holding of conferences. It is also the home of the Scottish Agricultural Museum. Part of the National Museums of Scotland, the museum illustrates the life and work of past generations on the land. There are displays of original farming tools, equipment, archive photographs and models.

EAST EDINBURGH

CRAIGMILLAR CASTLE

*M*OST people initially associate the name of Craigmillar with the location of one of the City of Edinburgh's modern housing estates. The housing estate, however, represents only the most recent chapter in a lengthy history, for Craigmillar can trace its story back some 700 years.

Craigmillar appears in the historical record of the thirteenth century because of its most durable building, Craigmillar Castle, now a substantial ruin, but in its time a stronghold that played an interesting role in Scotland's story. Craigmillar was, of course, situated far outside Edinburgh when James V, the father of Mary, Queen of Scots, resided there in 1517. Like every other building of any note, Craigmillar Castle suffered badly at the hands of the Earl of Hertford during the English invasion of 1544.

It was restored, however, and it was here that Mary, Queen of Scots took refuge

Craigmillar Castle

Craigmillar Castle

following the brutal murder of her secretary, David Rizzio, in March 1566. It is said, too, that Craigmillar was the spot at which the decision was taken to do away with the unfortunate Lord Darnley, Mary's husband, who was blown up at Kirk o' Field, Edinburgh, in February 1567.

Not far distant is Little France, a name that commemorates the considerable number of French courtiers and servants who had arrived from France with Mary and found accommodation near Craigmillar Castle.

In the main street of Newcraighall an impressive sculpture by Jake Harvey (1989) commemorates the coal mining communities which formerly flourished in this region, moulding the landscape and the character of its people.

SPORTING EDINBURGH

RECREATION FOR ALL

*T*HE sporting enthusiast will find a wealth of facilities available in Edinburgh.

For the swimmer, there is the splendid Royal Commonwealth Pool, in Holyrood Park Road, which was built for the 1970 Commonwealth Games. In addition to the main pool, in which competitions of international status are regularly held, there is a separate diving pool, a teaching pool and sauna facilities. A spectacular added attraction at the Commonwealth Pool is a flume,

or waterslide, in which the swimmer is propelled at speed along a variety of enclosed watercourses before being shot, exhilarated, into a pool.

The city's swimming facilities also include six neighbourhood swimming centres: these are at Caledonian Crescent, Dalry; Glenogle Road; Infirmary Street; Junction Place, Leith; Bellfield Street, Portobello; and Warrender, in Thirlestane Road.

The Edinburgh derby: Hearts v Hibs

Scotland v Zimbabwe

City-centre cycle race

Murrayfield Racers v Fife Flyers

There are a number of sports centres in the city, all operated by the City of Edinburgh District Council. The biggest is Meadowbank, in London Road, built for the 1970 Commonwealth Games (and again the principal venue when the Games returned to Edinburgh in 1986). Meadowbank regularly hosts sporting events at international level, for its excellent facilities extend to a number of indoor halls also. More than 80 sports can be catered for at Meadowbank throughout the year.

Craiglockhart Sports Centre, at no. 177 Colinton Road, has a delightful rural situation, a boating pond, and is noted for its tennis facilities. The tennis played at Craiglockhart includes tournaments at international level.

The modern Jack Kane Centre, which stands amid parkland at Niddrie Mains Road, is an important focal point in the life of Craigmillar. One half of this complex is a well-equipped sports centre, in which a wide programme of sports is available; the other half of the building is a community centre, which plays an active role in encouraging the arts.

At Saughton Park there is a multi-sports complex operated by the City of Edinburgh, while there are two further neighbourhood leisure centres, at Gracemount and Ainslie Park.

Golfers, as one would expect, are well catered for in Edinburgh. There are no fewer than six municipal courses, quite apart from the 28 private clubs within the city, many of whom also welcome visitors. The publicly owned courses are Braid Hills (two full courses); Carrick Knowe, at Balgreen Road; Craigentinny, at Craigentinny Avenue; Silverknowes, at Silverknowes Parkway; and Portobello (nine holes). In addition, there is a short-hole course at Bruntsfield Links, near Tollcross. At Fairview Road, Newbridge, the Port Royal Golf Range offers floodlit bays, practice bunkers,

Opposite: Braid Hills golf course

Ainslie Park Leisure Centre

a putting green and professional tuition.

Sailing on the Firth of Forth is available from a number of bases within the city boundaries. Port Edgar, near South Queensferry, has a first-class marina. There are walk-on pontoon berths usable at all states of the tide. Ashore, there is ample space for outdoor hardstanding and for some 150 yachts and dinghies in sheds. A cafeteria, picnic area and a woodland walk overlook the harbour. Cramond, at the mouth of the River Almond, is a popular spot with sailing enthusiasts, and Granton Harbour is the home of the Royal Forth Yacht Club.

All-year-round skiing is available at Hillend Park, situated a short distance south of Fairmilehead crossroads. In the park, which is on the slopes of the Pentland Hills, is an artificial ski slope that enables devotees to pursue their sport in summer as well as in winter. There is also a chairlift.

Murrayfield, Scotland's international rugby ground, has been developed by the Scottish Rugby Union into a first-class modern stadium. A short distance away, Murrayfield Ice Rink offers ice-skating and curling and is also the base of the ice hockey club, Murrayfield Racers.

Edinburgh's leading football clubs are Hearts, whose home, Tynecastle Park, is in Gorgie; Hibs, whose base at present is Easter Road Park, Albion Road; and Meadowbank Thistle, whose home fixtures are played at Meadowbank Sports Centre.

A number of sports, including football, rugby, hockey, tennis, squash, bowls, putting and cricket, are followed both in public parks and in private clubs.

For followers of horse racing, both on the flat and over fences, meetings are held regularly at Musselburgh, just beyond the Edinburgh city boundary.

THE MODERN CITY

EDINBURGH MEANS BUSINESS

*M*UCH of Edinburgh's charm stems from the way in which past and present live easily side by side. Diverted by the city's physical beauty, it is easy for the visitor to overlook the fact that Edinburgh is also a busy, thriving, modern community, providing a working and living environment for 440,000 people.

Less than one-fifth of the working population are employed in manufacturing industry. The rest are in a variety of service industries, so plainly the service sector is fundamental to the economic well-being of Edinburgh.

However, though manufacturing has declined in size in recent years, it remains important. The manufacturing sector in Edinburgh is dominated by three industrial groups, namely: electrical and electronics engineering; paper, printing and publishing; and food and drink. These three account for more than 75 per cent of all manufacturing

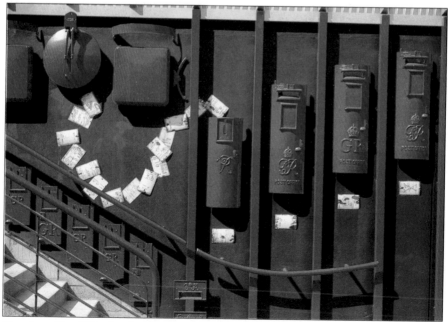

Postal art, Post Office Sorting Centre

employment.

In electrical and electronics engineering, the four leading companies are Hewlett Packard, Racal, NEI Peebles and GEC Marconi Avionics. Moreover, there is a growing number of small firms in the field of advanced technology who, as well as showing employment growth, are providing a vital research resource for the wider sector.

The City of Edinburgh District Council's economic strategy includes

Business development at South Gyle

support for the development of new technologies and their application. Edinburgh University, Heriot-Watt University and Napier University are all at the forefront of a number of leading-edge technologies, and the Technology Transfer Centre at Edinburgh University, conducting research which can be developed for commercial application, provides an example of a beneficial joint venture between city and university.

Edinburgh's economic strengths are in electronics, information technology, tourism and financial services. The importance of financial services, which has always been considerable in Edinburgh, continues to grow. Indeed, financial services now take up about a third of all commercial office space in the city.

Edinburgh has always enjoyed a good reputation for handling other people's money, and in the context of the United Kingdom, Edinburgh's importance as a financial centre is second only to that of London. Scottish Financial Enterprise, an organisation which was formed to represent the community of banks, insurance groups, fund managers and financial services companies, has more than 200 members, of whom almost half have their head office in Edinburgh. The objective of this organisation is to help the financial community to grow and to benefit from opportunities arising in the wake of the world-wide deregulation of financial services.

Edinburgh has two major industrial estates, both on the west side of the city. The older of the two has been established at Sighthill for more than 40 years; the second, at Gyle, is still growing. More than two million square feet of business, retail, leisure and residential space will have easy access to road, rail and air transport, and the development will also have the world's most advanced telecommunications. It all means that west Edinburgh is blossoming into one of Europe's most exciting business locations.

New West Edinburgh (four miles from the city centre, and just two miles from Edinburgh International Airport) will have everything from sites to purpose-built office developments. The development includes Scotland's largest and most ambitious commercial development, the 138-acre Edinburgh Park – a joint venture between the Miller Group and Edinburgh Development and Investment (a City of Edinburgh District Council subsidiary). When completed, the park will offer high technology and financial services headquarter buildings, with landscaping that includes a central water feature. The park will have its own access to the M8 extension (due to be completed in early 1995) and to the Edinburgh City Bypass, which provides a gateway to the entire UK motorway network.

Good telecommunications are crucial

Opposite: The Trustee Savings Bank Head Office

SHOPPING

Cunningham & Co., North St Andrew St

D. Napier & Sons, Bristo Place

Valvona and Crolla, Elm Row

Round the World, West Bow

Now and Then, West Crosscauseway

Lighting Emporium, Stockbridge

EDINBURGH

Whytock & Reid, Belford Mews

Herrald Antiques, Queen Street

Wind Things, Grassmarket

Candle Shop, Candlemaker Row

The Pipe Shop, Leith Walk

West Pier Motor Cycles, Brandon Terrace

S H O P P I N G

Forbidden Planet, Teviot Place

Cadenhead Whisky Shop, Canongate

Aika, High Street

J.E. Hogg, Wine Merchant, Cumberland Street

Robert Cresser, West Bow

Score Commotions, West Bow

EDINBURGH

Iain Mellis, Cheesemonger, West Bow

R. Somerville, Playing Cards, Canongate

Charles MacSween & Co., Bruntsfield Place

James Casey, St Mary's Street

Clan Bagpipes, Lawnmarket

Mr Wood's Fossils, Grassmarket

The Edinburgh International Conference Centre under construction

to international business, and so Edinburgh is equipped with the United Kingdom's first major integrated digital telephone network based on fibre optics. Edinburgh enjoys instantaneous access to every form of electronic communication currently available in the world. Access to satellite communication links and video-conferencing facilities are also available.

A major shopping centre development by the City of Edinburgh, Marks and Spencer and Safeway was opened at the Gyle, adjacent to Edinburgh Park, in 1993.

Edinburgh International Airport, which is only eight miles from the city centre, is served by 11 airlines flying to 27 destinations. There are hourly flights to London, making it easy to connect to destinations world-wide. There are direct flights from Edinburgh to Paris, Amsterdam, Brussels and Dublin.

Edinburgh's commitment to the sciences in general and new technologies in particular is further demonstrated at the annual Edinburgh International Science Festival. Held in April each year, it brings together all scientific disciplines. It unites everyone with an interest in science, from local children to international research biologists, from companies adopting new technologies to individuals concerned about the environment. The Science Festival focuses attention on the issues and advances of science through conferences, seminars, lectures, exhibitions, demonstrations and popular events.

As well as being Britain's most popular holiday destination after London, Edinburgh is a favourite venue for conferences of all types and sizes. The Edinburgh International Conference Centre, Morrison Street, is due to open in 1995. It will provide international-standard, purpose-built meeting facilities of the highest quality, right in the heart of the city. The unique feature of the centre is the main auditorium. Providing raked seating for 1,200 delegates theatre-style, the auditorium can be quickly sub-divided into three separate, self-contained auditoria for 600, 300 and 300. Supported by exhibition and catering areas and a range of break-out rooms, the centre will also offer the latest in presentation and communications technology. Adjacent to the conference centre will be another development, providing one million sq. ft of high-quality office space and creating a new

and Chinese. There are also excellent fish restaurants, particularly in Leith. Edinburgh is also noted for its pubs, a number of which are celebrated for their elegant Victorian and Edwardian interiors.

There are many attractive shops in Edinburgh. These range from the spacious and well-ordered department stores of Princes Street, George Street and the West End, to the informality of the antique shop. These antique shops are encountered

'World Markets', Crewe Toll

business district in the heart of the city. Edinburgh has more than 15,000 beds available in a wide range of hotel accommo-dation, up to five-star, as well as a large number of comfortable guest-houses.

Good restaurants abound, many of them being featured in national good food guides. The cuisine available is interna-tional: ethnic restaurants include French, Italian, Swiss, Spanish, Indian, Pakistani,

throughout Edinburgh, but they will be found in concentration in the New Town around Stockbridge, Thistle Street and North West Circus Place; and in the Old Town in Causewayside, Victoria Street and the Grassmarket. Who can resist the appeal, the inherent mystery of the antique shop? To enter a department store may be interesting, but to enter an antique shop is an adventure.

INDEX

I N D E X

I N D E X

I N D E X

INDEX